# The Constitutional Law Dictionary

# THE CONSTITUTIONAL LAW DICTIONARY

# VOLUME 1: INDIVIDUAL RIGHTS

Supplement 1

Covering the 1983–84, 1984–85, and 1985–86 Terms of the Supreme Court

Ralph C. Chandler
Richard A. Enslen
Peter G. Renstrom

**ABC-CLIO**

Santa Barbara, California
Oxford, England

**Library of Congress Cataloging in Publication Data**

Chandler, Ralph C., 1934–
    The constitutional law dictionary.

    Vol. 1. kept up to date by supplements.
    Includes index.
    Contents: v. 1. Individual rights.
    1. United States—Constitutional law—Terms and phases.   2. United States—Constitutional law—Cases.
    I. Enslen, Richard A., 1931–        II. Renstrom,
    Peter G., 1943–      . III. Title.
    KF4548.5.C47   1985        342.73      84-12320
                               347.302
    ISBN 0–87436–484–1

    10   9   8   7   6   5   4   3   2   1   (cloth)


*Cover design by Tanya Cullen*


ABC-Clio, Inc.
2040 Alameda Padre Serra, Box 4397
Santa Barbara, California 93140-4397

Clio Press Ltd.
55 St. Thomas Street
Oxford, OX1 1JG, England


This book is printed on acid-free paper ⊗.
Manufactured in the United States of America

# Clio Dictionaries in Political Science

*The African Political Dictionary*
Claude S. Phillips

*The Asian Political Dictionary*
Lawrence Ziring

*The Constitutional Law Dictionary,* Volume 1: *Individual Rights*
Ralph C. Chandler, Richard A. Enslen, and Peter G. Renstrom

*The Constitutional Law Dictionary,* Volume 1: *Individual Rights,*
Supplement 1
Ralph C. Chandler, Richard A. Enslen, and Peter G. Renstrom

*The Dictionary of Political Analysis,* Second Edition
Jack C. Plano, Robert E. Riggs, and Helenan S. Robin

*The European Political Dictionary*
Ernest E. Rossi and Barbara P. McCrea

*The International Law Dictionary*
Robert L. Bledsoe and Boleslaw A. Boczek

*The Latin American Political Dictionary*
Ernest E. Rossi and Jack C. Plano

*The Middle East Political Dictionary*
Lawrence Ziring

*The Presidential-Congressional Political Dictionary*
Jeffrey M. Elliot and Sheikh R. Ali

*The Public Policy Dictionary*
Earl R. Kruschke and Byron M. Jackson

*The Soviet and East European Political Dictionary*
Barbara P. McCrea, Jack C. Plano, and George Klein

# The Constitutional Law Dictionary

## Forthcoming

*The Arms Control, Disarmament, and Military Security Dictionary*
Jeffrey M. Elliot and Robert Reginald

*The Constitutional Law Dictionary,* Volume 2: *Governmental Powers*
Ralph C. Chandler, Richard A. Enslen, and Peter G. Renstrom

*The International Relations Dictionary,* Fourth Edition
Jack C. Plano and Roy Olton

*The State and Local Government Political Dictionary*
Jeffrey M. Elliot and Sheikh R. Ali

# SERIES STATEMENT

Language precision is the primary tool of every scientific discipline. That aphorism serves as the guideline for this series of political dictionaries. Although each book in the series relates to a specific topical or regional area in the discipline of political science, entries in the dictionaries also emphasize history, geography, economics, sociology, philosophy, and religion.

This dictionary series incorporates special features designed to help the reader overcome any language barriers that may impede a full understanding of the subject matter. For example, the concepts included in each volume were selected to complement the subject matter found in existing texts and other books. All but one volume utilize a subject-matter chapter arrangement that is most useful for classroom and study purposes.

Entries in all volumes include an up-to-date definition plus a paragraph of *Significance* in which the authors discuss and analyze each term's historical and current relevance. Most entries are also cross-referenced, providing the reader an opportunity to seek additional information related to the subject of inquiry. A comprehensive index, found in both hardcover and paperback editions, allows the reader to locate major entries and other concepts, events, and institutions discussed within these entries.

The political and social sciences suffer more than most disciplines from semantic confusion. This is attributable, *inter alia,* to the popularization of the language, and to the focus on many diverse foreign political and social systems. This dictionary series is dedicated to overcoming some of this confusion through careful writing of thorough, accurate definitions for the central concepts, institutions, and events that comprise the basic knowledge of each of the subject fields. New titles in the series will be issued periodically, including some in related social science disciplines.

— Jack C. Plano
*Series Editor*

# CONTENTS

# A NOTE ON HOW TO USE THIS BOOK

Students of constitutional law know the extent to which the law is ever changing. With each new term of the Supreme Court the justices review their previous decisions and those of their predecessors in light of current legal and social circumstances. The changes that are made are frequently incremental: a nuance here and an adjustment there. The Court may wish simply to apply an established doctrine or more clearly define a standard in a particular case as it weighs real-world situations on the scales of justice. Sometimes it sweeps aside an entire line of precedent in a bold new interpretation of the Constitution. The system is constantly in flux. It is evolutionary, developmental, and responsive to human need. Thus it adds stability to the governmental system as a whole. A systems theorist would say constitutional law has a well-defined dynamic feedback loop.

These conditions create certain problems for writers and publishers of constitutional law books. Given the lead time necessary to prepare such a book, it is out of date in some particulars on the day it is published. In this case, *The Constitutional Law Dictionary,* Volume 1: *Individual Rights,* was published in early 1985. The material in it had to be completed in the spring of 1984, during the middle of the 1983–84 term of the Supreme Court. Significant decisions yet to be made in that term, plus the entire 1984–85 and 1985–86 terms, are therefore not included in the book.

To remedy the obvious need to update the general reader and researcher, this supplement is offered as the Court begins its 1986–87 term. The following guidelines apply:

(1) Chapters 1 and 8 of the original work are not affected. "Constitutionalism" and "Legal Words and Phrases" remain intact as previously published.

(2) The other six chapters are moved up one chapter number each in the contents listing of the supplement. In the original work the First Amendment was Chapter 2, following "Constitutionalism." In the current work it is Chapter 1, and so forth.

(3) All *See also* page number references are keyed to the original work. It is therefore a good idea to have the original work at hand when using the supplement.

(4) Rather than include parts of cases that have been modified since publication of the original work, the entire case is included in the supplement and represents the matter as it now stands in constitutional law. When a new case has replaced an older one, as *Batson v. Kentucky* (90 L.Ed. 2d 69: 1986) replaced *Swain v. Alabama* (380 U.S. 202: 1965) on the matter of jury selection, for example, the new standards have been noted in the *Significance* section of the discussion. The alphabetical list of case entries at the beginning of the supplement assembles all of the 109 new cases appearing for the first time, plus the older cases they modify. The reader should bear in mind that in most instances the new cases are introduced in the descriptions of these older cases, which are also listed at the beginning of each chapter with the new cases mentioned under them. When an asterisk appears before a case, as it does 16 times, a complete new entry is indicated. These new cases frequently overturn previously established court doctrine.

(5) In some instances the complete case citation is unavailable because reference page numbers have not yet been assigned by the official publisher of the cases. This is particularly true of 1986 cases, where the complete citation is available only in the Lawyers Edition of the decisions we have included.

We are gratified by the good reception *The Constitutional Law Dictionary* has received, and we hope this supplement will make the book even more useful.

— Ralph C. Chandler
Professor of Political Science
*Western Michigan University*

— Richard A. Enslen
United States District Judge
*Western District of Michigan*

— Peter G. Renstrom
Professor of Political Science
*Western Michigan University*

# ALPHABETICAL LIST OF CASE ENTRIES

# The Constitutional Law Dictionary

# 1. The First Amendment

## Free Speech, 16

## Free Press, 18

## Assembly and Protest, 31

## Association, 33

# ESTABLISHMENT OF RELIGION
## Moment of Silence

*Wallace v. Jaffree*, **472 U.S. 38, 105 S.Ct. 2479, 86 L.Ed. 2d 29 (1985)** Struck down a state statute authorizing a moment of silence to be used for meditation or voluntary prayer in public schools. *Wallace v. Jaffree* began as a challenge to three statutes in the state of Alabama. The first was enacted in 1978 and authorized a one-minute period of silence in all public schools "for meditation." The second was passed in 1981 and provided for a period of silence "for meditation or voluntary prayer." In 1982 Alabama adopted yet another statute allowing teachers to lead "willing students" in prayer at the beginning of class. The 1982 statute prescribed that the prayer be to "Almighty God the Creator and Supreme Judge of the World." A United States District Court found no defect in the 1978 law, but ruled the other two statutes to be an attempt by the state to encourage religious activity. Nonetheless the District Court said the state could so establish religion if it wished. Review was sought from the Court of Appeals which agreed that the 1978 statute was permissible, but held the 1981 and 1982 statutes to be unconstitutional. Alabama pursued appeals. The Supreme Court summarily affirmed the Court of Appeals holding on the 1982 statute and agreed to review the 1981 statute in more detail. The decision in *Wallace* is therefore confined to the moment of silence issue. In a 6–3 decision, the Court held the 1981 statute to be unconstitutional. Justice Stevens delivered the opinion of the Court. He said the right to speech and the right to refrain from speaking are "complementary components of a broader concept of individual freedom of mind." The right to "choose his own creed" is the counterpart of one's right to "refrain from accepting the creed established by the majority." Stevens said the Court historically had unambiguously conceded that the freedom of conscience protected by the First Amendment "embraces the right to select any religious faith or none at all." This conclusion derives support not only from protection of the interest of freedom of conscience, but also from the view that "religious beliefs worthy of respect are the product of free and voluntary choice by the faithful." Stevens

7

affirmed use of the criteria in *Lemon v. Kurtzman* (403 U.S. 602: 1971) for Establishment Clause cases. These standards call for challenged legislation to pass a three-pronged test: (1) the statute must have a secular purpose; (2) its principal or primary effect may not advance or inhibit religion; and (3) the statute must not foster an "excessive governmental entanglement" with religion. Stevens said the first of these criteria is "most plainly implicated" by *Wallace*. In applying the secular purpose test, Stevens argued that it was appropriate to ask whether government's actual purpose is to endorse or disapprove of religion. The legislative record provided an unambiguous affirmative answer at this point. It showed the bill's sponsor to say that the law was "an effort to return voluntary school prayer" to the public schools of Alabama. The Court also based its conclusion on a comparison of the relevant Alabama statutes. The only significant difference between the 1978 and 1981 laws, for example, was the addition of the words "or voluntary prayer." This was done, said Stevens, to convey a message of state endorsement and promotion of prayer. Addition of the words "or voluntary prayer" indicated that the state "intended to characterize prayer as a favored practice." Such an endorsement was not consistent with the principle that government must pursue a course of complete neutrality toward religion. Justice O'Connor offered a concurring opinion which distinguished the defective Alabama law from those laws which simply call for a moment of silence. The latter do not deal with an exercise which is "inherently religious," she said, and the participating student "need not compromise his or her beliefs." O'Connor argued that when a state mandates a moment of silence, it does not necessarily "endorse any activity that might occur during the period." The dissenters in *Wallace* were Chief Justice Burger and Justices White and Rehnquist. Burger took an accommodationist stance, saying simply the law did not create an established religion. The statute only endorsed the view that religious observance "should be tolerated, and, where possible, accommodated." Burger said the Court's decision "manifests not neutrality but hostility toward religion." Rehnquist attacked the "wall of separation" metaphor frequently used in establishment cases, saying it was based on bad history and had proven useless as a guide. He saw the Establishment Clause as prohibiting only the designation of a national church or giving preference to one sect or denomination over another. Accordingly, the clause did not preclude government from giving nondiscriminatory encouragement to religion. Neither did it require governmental neutrality between religion and irreligion. *See also* ENGEL V. VITALE (370 U.S. 421: 1962), p. 84; ESTABLISHMENT CLAUSE, p. 408; *LEMON V. KURTZMAN* (403 U.S. 602: 1971), p. 92.

*Significance*　　The Court refused to allow a moment of silence law in *Wallace v. Jaffree* (472 U.S. 38: 1985) because it saw the statute as conveying a message of endorsement and promotion of religion. The decision was a strong reiteration of the Court's position in *Engel v. Vitale* (370 U.S. 421: 1962, p. 84), which prohibited the recital of a state-composed prayer by public school students. *Wallace* also reaffirmed the establishment tests fashioned by the Court in *Lemon v. Kurtzman* (403 U.S. 602: 1971, p. 92) and other school aid cases. Thus the Court seemed to turn away from what many observers thought was a drift toward a more accommodationist position, illustrated in the nativity scene case of *Lynch v. Donnelly* (79 L.Ed. 2d 604: 1984). In *Lynch* a municipality had included a crèche in its Christmas celebration display. When the crèche was challenged as a violation of the Establishment Clause, the Court resisted the challenge in a 5–4 decision, saying it had consistently rejected a "rigid, absolutist view" of the clause throughout its history. Furthermore, it was not completely accurate to speak of a wall of separation dividing church and state. "Our society cannot have segments or institutions which exist in a vacuum or in total isolation from all the other parts, much less from government." The Court maintained that history shows unbroken acknowledgment of the role of religion in American life, and the crèche scene merely depicted the historical origins of Christmas. If the crèche scene benefited religion at all, it was only in an "indirect, remote, and incidental fashion." The Court concluded that the city's motives for including the crèche were secular, that religion was not impermissibly advanced, and that an excessive entanglement of religion and government was not created. *Wallace v. Jaffree* then returned to a stricter separation of church and state than *Lynch v. Donnelly* had seemed to presage.

## Aid to Nonpublic Schools

***Lemon v. Kurtzman*, 403 U.S. 602, 91 S.Ct. 2105, 29 L.Ed. 2d 745 (1971)**　　Prohibited salary supplements for nonpublic schoolteachers. *Lemon* involved a Pennsylvania statute which authorized reimbursement to nonpublic schools for expenditures "for teachers, textbooks, and instructional materials." The reimbursement was limited to "courses presented in the curricula of the public schools." A school seeking reimbursement needed to identify the separate costs of the eligible "secular educational service." The contested statute specifically prohibited reimbursement for "any course that contains 'any subject matter expressing religious teaching, or the morals or forms of worship of any sect.'" The Supreme Court struck down the statute in a unanimous decision, with Justice Marshall not participating, on the ground that the statute fostered an "excessive entanglement with religion." In assessing the entanglement question, the Court indicated it must "examine the character and purposes of the institutions which are benefitted, the nature of aid that the State provides, and the resulting relationship between the government and the religious authority." The main problem was the "ideological character" of teachers. The Court could not "ignore the dangers that a teacher under religious control and discipline poses to the separation of the religious from the purely secular aspects of precollege education." Although parochial teachers may not intentionally violate First Amendment proscriptions, "a dedicated religious person, teaching in a school affiliated with his or her faith and operated to inculcate its tenets, will inevitably experience great difficulty in remaining religiously neutral." If a state is to make reimbursements available, it must be certain that subsidized teachers do not inculcate religion. The comprehensive and continuing surveillance required to maintain that limit itself becomes an establishment defect since the "prophylactic contacts will involve excessive and enduring entanglement between state and church." Ongoing inspection of school records is a "relationship pregnant with dangers of excessive government direction in church schools." Finally, the Court found entanglement of a different character created by the "divisive political potential of state programs." Continuation of such state assistance will "entail considerable political activity." While political debate is normally a "healthy manifestation of our democratic system . . . political division along religious lines was one of the principal evils against which the First Amendment was intended to protect." *See also* CPEARL V. NYQUIST (413 U.S. 756: 1973), p. 94; FIRST AMENDMENT, p. 77; *TILTON V. RICHARDSON* (403 U.S. 672: 1971), p. 82; *WOLMAN V. WALTER* (433 U.S. 406: 1977), p. 96.

*Significance*        *Lemon v. Kurtzman* (403 U.S. 602: 1971) clearly reflected the decisive role of the entanglement criterion in establishment cases. The Burger Court's reliance on that criterion did not diminish. The Court again noted the difference between precollege levels of education and higher education as it had defined the distinction in *Tilton*. Religious indoctrination is only an incidental purpose of education at the college level, while educational objectives at the lower levels have a "substantial religious character." *Lemon* emphasizes that the Court sees programs at the elementary and secondary levels as inherently susceptible to entanglement problems. *Lemon* also casts serious doubt on purchase-of-service programs. Monitoring personnel, especially teachers, would be an ongoing obligation which would excessively entangle government and the church school. Transportation and books, on the other hand, have no content to be evaluated or they are subject only to a one-time review. Service items are much more difficult to fit into child benefit coverage than are books and transportation. *Lemon* involved an irresolvable establishment problem. Religion would obviously be advanced in violation of the purpose and effects criteria without the surveillance of teachers. At the same time, the maintenance of a monitoring system produces entanglement defects. *Lemon* added another dimension to the entanglement test. As nonpublic schools encounter greater financial difficulty, demands to retain or expand aid programs will grow and communities will be divided along religious lines. Such community divisiveness is an end the Establishment Clause must seek to avoid. The Court reaffirmed the *Lemon* ruling in two shared-time cases in 1985. In *Grand Rapids School District v. Ball* (87 L.Ed. 2d 267: 1985) and *Aguilar v. Felton* (87 L.Ed. 2d 290: 1985), it struck down programs in public school systems which sent teachers into nonpublic schools to provide remedial instruction. These programs were seen as advancing religion and fostering an excessively entangled relationship between government and religion. The Court said that state-paid teachers, "influenced by the pervasively sectarian nature of the religious schools in which they work," may subtly or overtly indoc-trinate students with particular religious views at public expense. The symbolic union of church and state inherent in the provision of secular, state-provided instruction in religious school buildings "threatens to convey a message of state support for religion." The Court said the effect of the programs is to subsidize the religious functions of the parochial schools by taking over a substantial portion of the responsibil-ity for secular subjects. The "conveying a message" criterion was coupled with the "student benefit" doctrine in *Witters v. Washington Department of Services for the Blind* (88 L.Ed. 2d 846: 1986). Witters suffered from a condition which made him eligible for state vocational rehabilitation assistance for blind persons. He sought such assistance to cover the costs of his studies at a Christian college where he was engaged in a program leading to a religious vocation. The aid was denied on the ground that public money could not be used to obtain religious instruction. The Court ruled, however, that such aid did not advance religion. The aid was given directly to Witters and any money which eventually gets to religious institutions in these circumstances comes as a result of the "genuinely independent and private choices of the aid recipients." That Witters chose to use the aid in this way did not confer any message of state endorsement of religion.

# FREE EXERCISE OF RELIGION

## Conscientious Objection: Draft

*Gillette v. United States*, 401 U.S. 437, 91 S.Ct. 828, 28 L.Ed. 2d 168 (1971) Held that a religion-based objection to a particular war, as distinct from wars generally, does not entitle a person to exemption from the military draft. *Gillette* examined the specific language of the Selective Service Act, particularly that part of the act which exempted registrants who are "conscientiously opposed to participation in war in any form." Gillette had attempted to limit his objection to participation in the Vietnam War, but the Supreme Court, with only Justice Douglas dissenting, held he was not entitled to such a free exercise exemption. The Court also determined that Congress could provide exemptions to the draft for those having religion-based objections to wars generally without violating establishment prohibitions. While conscription of those with "conscientious scruples" against all wars would violate the free exercise proscription, there are governmental interests of "sufficient kind and weight" to justify drafting people who object to particular wars. The Court determined that the draft laws were not "designed to interfere with any religious ritual or practice and do not work a penalty against any theological position." In addition, the burdens imposed are incidental when compared to the substantial government interest in creating and administering an equitable exemption policy. The Court also noted the interest of the government in "procuring the manpower necessary for military purposes." These interests permit what Gillette alleged to be an interference with his free exercise rights. The establishment claim was based on the argument that allowing exemption only to those with objection to all wars discriminated against faiths which "distinguish between personal participation in 'just' and 'unjust' wars." The Court held that congressional objectives in requiring objection to all wars were neutral, secular, and did not reflect a religious preference. The Court focused on the need for the exemption to have a neutral basis. Since a virtually "limitless variety of beliefs are subsumable under the rubric 'objection to a particular war,'" the difficulties of operating a fair and uniform conscription system would be substantial. Sorting through the various claims creates a great "potential for state involvement in determining the character of persons' beliefs and affiliations, thus 'entangling government in difficult classifications of what is or is not religious,' or what is or is not conscientious." Acknowledging that some discretion exists under any process which takes individual differences into account, the Court found that establishment problems would be even greater if conscientious objection of indeterminate scope was involved. *See also* BILL OF RIGHTS, p. 7; FIRST AMENDMENT, p. 77; *SHERBERT V. VERNER* (374 U.S. 398: 1964), p. 103.

*Significance*    *Gillette v. United States* (401 U.S. 437: 1971) was unique in singling out a particular war for religion-based conscientious objection to an American draft law. The Selective Service and Training Act of 1940 provided that conscientious objector status did not require affiliation with a religious sect. The claim of exemption required only theistic religious beliefs and training, and not a "merely personal moral code." The Court addressed this language in *United States v. Seeger* (380 U.S. 163: 1965), holding a conscientious objector claimant need not declare a belief in a Supreme Being as long as the claimant had beliefs which served in the place of an orthodox belief in God. The term *Supreme Being* was said to mean a broader view of something to which everything else is subordinate. In *Welsh v. United States* (398 U.S. 333: 1970), the Court required exemption for a claimant without the basis of his objections resting on religious training or belief as long as the claimant genuinely believed in pacifism. A selective conscientious objector such as Gillette, on the other hand, created problems of implementation so wrought with establishment defects as to outweigh the free exercise interest served by the exemption. More recent chapters were written on this issue in *Rostker v. Goldberg* (453 U.S. 57: 1981), *Selective Service System v. Minnesota Public Interest Research Group* (468 U.S. 841: 1984), and *Wayte v. United States* (470 U.S. 598: 1985). *Rostker* upheld a 1980 presidential proclamation issued pursuant to the Military Selective Service Act requiring every male citizen and resident alien to register for potential conscription. In the *Minnesota Public Interest Research Group* case, the Court permitted denial of federal student aid to persons failing to register for the draft, saying the policy had been aimed at securing compliance rather than seeking punishment of nonregistrants. The policy had been challenged on bill of attainder, self-incrimination, and equal protection grounds. In *Wayte,* the Court allowed the temporary use of a passive enforcement of the draft registration law, whereby initial prosecutions were undertaken only against those nonregistrants who publicized their resistance to the policy or were reported by others to be in violation. The Court said such an approach would be impermissible only if discriminating motive and effect could be shown.

## Unemployment Compensation

**Sherbert v. Verner, 374 U.S. 398, 83 S.Ct. 1790, 10 L.Ed. 2d 965 (1963)**    Held that a state may not disqualify a person from unemployment compensation because the person refuses to work on Saturdays for religious reasons. *Sherbert* said the protection of free exercise interests may produce an exemption from secular regulation based on religion. Sherbert was a Seventh-Day Adventist who was discharged from her job because she would not work on Saturday. Saturday is the Sabbath Day for Adventists. Failing to find other employment because of her "conscientious scruples not to take Saturday work," Sherbert filed for unemployment compensation benefits under provisions of South Carolina law. The law required that any claimant is ineligible for benefits if he or she has failed, without good cause, to accept suitable work when offered. Through appropriate administrative proceedings, Sherbert's unwillingness to work on Saturdays was determined to disqualify her from benefits. The Supreme Court held for Sherbert in a 7–2 decision. The burdens imposed on her in this case were too great. She was forced to choose between "following the precepts of her religion and forfeiting benefits," or "abandoning one of the precepts of her religion in order to accept work." Facing such a choice "puts the same kind of burden upon the free exercise of religion as would a fine imposed against appellant for her Saturday worship." The Court failed to find that protection of the unemployment compensation fund from fraudulent claims by unscrupulous claimants feigning religious objections to Saturday work was a sufficiently compelling state interest. Even if the fund were threatened by spurious claims, South Carolina would need to demonstrate that no alternative forms of regulation would combat such abuses. In requiring the religion-based exemption for Sherbert, the Court imposed a requirement of possible differential treatment for those seeking unemployment benefits for refusal to work on Saturdays. The Court suggested, however, that such classification was not the establishment of religion. The decision "reflects nothing more than the governmental obligation of neutrality in the face of religious differences." The holding requires only that "South Carolina may not constitutionally apply the eligibility provisions so as to constrain a worker to abandon his religious convictions." Justices Harlan and White dissented on the ground that the decision required an exemption based upon religion. The decision requires South Carolina to "single out for financial assistance those whose behavior is religiously motivated, even though it denies such assistance to others whose identical behavior (in this case, inability to work on Saturdays) is not religiously motivated." See also FIRST AMENDMENT, p. 77; GILLETTE V. UNITED STATES (401 U.S. 437: 1971), p. 105; SUNDAY CLOSING LAW CASES (366 U.S. 421: 1961), p. 101; WISCONSIN V. YODER (406 U.S. 205: 1971), p. 106.

*Significance*    Sherbert v. Verner (374 U.S. 398: 1964) was something of a replay of the free exercise issues seen in *Braunfeld* and *Crown Kosher Supermarket*. Sherbert was subjected to economic hardship, like the merchants in the *Sunday Closing Cases*, but the burden in the *Sunday Closing Cases* was indirect. In *Sherbert* the Court found the burden to be impermissibly heavy. Even incidental burdens could be justified only by demonstrating a compelling state interest. The compelling interest criterion is far more demanding than merely showing secular purpose. Coupled with the alternate means requirement carried over from the *Sunday Closing Cases, Sherbert* substantially expanded the protection afforded by the Free Exercise Clause. At the same time, the broadened protection for free exercise produces serious establishment questions. They can be seen clearly in *Thomas v. Review Board of the Indiana Employment Security Division* (450 U.S. 707: 1981). Thomas was denied unemployment compensation after voluntarily quitting his job for religious reasons. The Court held the denial of benefits to be a violation of Thomas' free exercise rights. Only Justice Rehnquist dissented. The Court was even more emphatic than in *Sherbert*, saying, "Where the state conditions receipt of an important benefit upon conduct proscribed by religious faith, or where it denies such a benefit because of conduct mandated by religious belief," a believer is unduly pressured and a burden upon religion exists. While the compulsion may be indirect, the infringement upon free exercise is nonetheless substantial. Justice Rehnquist was wholly dissatisfied with the Court's preferential treatment of Thomas. He noted the Establishment Clause would preclude Indiana from legislating an unemployment compensation law with the exemption stipulated by the Court. He argued that the balance had now tipped too heavily in favor of free exercise protection. *Thomas* "reads the Free Exercise Clause too broadly and it fails to squarely acknowledge that such a reading conflicts with our Establishment Clause cases." As such, the decision simply exacerbates the tension between the two clauses. The Court took a step back from *Thomas* and *Sherbert* in *Estate of Thornton v. Caldor, Inc.* (86 L.Ed. 2d 557: 1985), invalidating a state law which gave any employee the absolute right to refuse to work on his or her Sabbath. The Court said the statute failed the primary effect test of *Lemon v. Kurtzman* (403 U.S. 602: 1971) in that it required religious concerns automatically to control all secular interests in the workplace. The following year the Court considered an Air Force uniform regulation which prohibited the wearing of headgear while on indoor duty. The regulation interfered with the wearing of a yarmulke by an officer who was an Orthodox Jew and an ordained rabbi and who served on indoor duty as a psychologist at a mental health clinic. In *Goldman v. Weinberger* (89 L.Ed. 2d 478: 1986), the Court held that the Free Exercise Clause does not require the military to accommodate such practices. The Court said the regulation operates reasonably and evenhandedly despite the burden imposed on this particular officer. Similarly, the Court maintained in *Bowen v. Roy* (90 L.Ed. 2d 735: 1986) that the Free Exercise Clause did not prevent the federal government from making social security numbers a condition for receipt of certain benefits such as food stamps and aid to dependent children. This holds even though obtaining such numbers may violate certain Indian religious beliefs. In this case a child's parents believed the numbers were evil and if widely used by the government would rob the spirit of their child. The Court said the Free Exercise Clause could not be interpreted as requiring the government to administer its internal affairs in ways that always comport with the religious beliefs of particular citizens.

# FREE SPEECH

## Overbreadth Doctrine

*Village of Schaumburg v. Citizens for a Better Environment,* **444 U.S. 620, 100 S.Ct. 826, 63 L.Ed. 2d 73 (1980)**        Struck down a local ordinance using the doctrine of overbreadth. In *Village of Schaumburg* the Supreme Court examined a local ordinance which prohibited door-to-door solicitations for contributions by organizations not using at least 75 percent of their receipts for charitable purposes. A charitable purpose excluded such items as salaries, overhead, solicitation costs, and other administrative expenses. An environmental group was denied permission to solicit because it could not demonstrate compliance with the 75 percent requirement. The organization sued, claiming First Amendment violations. The Court struck down the ordinance over the single dissent of Justice Rehnquist. The Court's primary objection was the overbreadth of the ordinance. The Court noted that a class of organizations existed to which the 75 percent rule could not constitutionally be applied. These were organizations "whose primary purpose is not to provide money or services to the poor, the needy, or other worthy objects of charity, but to gather and disseminate information about and advocate positions on matters of public concern." The costs of research, advocacy, or public education are typically in excess of 25 percent of funds raised. The Court felt that to lump all organizations failing to meet the 75 percent standard together imposed a direct and substantial limitation on protected activity. While the village interest in preventing fraud may generally be legitimate, the means to accomplish that end must use more precise measures to separate one kind from the other. *See also* BILL OF RIGHTS, p. 7; FIRST AMENDMENT, p. 77.

*Significance*    *Village of Schaumburg v. Citizens for a Better Environment*
(444 U.S. 620: 1980) is important because it produced a requirement
that statutes distinguish sufficiently between lawful and unlawful expression or behavior. In *Coates v. Cincinnati* (402 U.S. 611: 1971), the
Court struck down a city ordinance that prohibited three or more
persons from assembling on public sidewalks and conducting themselves in such a way as to "annoy any police officer or other persons who
should happen to pass by." The Court found the ordinance "makes a
crime out of what under the Constitution cannot be a crime." It was also
impermissibly vague. It conveyed no standard of conduct and "men of
common intelligence must necessarily guess at its meaning." Although
the overbreadth and vagueness doctrines have often been invoked to
invalidate enactments as in *Schaumburg* and *Coates*, some ordinances
survive such challenges. In *Grayned v. Rockford* (408 U.S. 104: 1972), the
Court allowed an antinoise ordinance prohibiting disturbances in the
proximity of schools in session. The specific school context separated
the restriction from the typically vague and general breach of the peace
ordinance. The enactment was seen as a reasonable time, place, and
manner restriction. It was narrowly tailored to further Rockford's
compelling interest in having undisrupted school sessions and was not
an impermissibly broad prophylactic. In *Village of Hoffman Estates v.
Flipside, Inc.* (456 U.S. 950: 1982), the Court upheld an ordinance
requiring a license to sell items designed or marketed for use with
illegal cannabis or drugs against claims that the ordinance was both
vague and overbroad. The Court ruled that the ordinance merely
sought to regulate the commercial marketing of illegal drug parapher-
nalia and did not reach noncommercial speech. The only potential limit
on Flipside's conveying of information was confined to the commercial
activity related to illegal drug use. The Court also found the vagueness
claim unpersuasive. The "designed for use" provision of the ordinance
covered at least some of the items sold at *Flipside*. The "marketed for
use" language provided ample warning to the retailer about licensure
and the display practices which could produce violation of the ordinance. The *Schaumberg* reasoning was later applied to a state limitation
on charity fund-raising expenses in *Secretary of State of Maryland v. J. H.
Munson Company* (467 U.S. 947: 1984). Maryland had enacted a statute
designed to prevent abusive and fradulent fund-raising by prohibiting
a charity from spending more than 25 percent of its gross income for
expenses. The Court invalidated the law, saying fund-raising for
charities was so intertwined with speech that it required First Amendment protection. The Maryland statute was based on the "fundamentally mistaken premise" that fund-raising costs that exceed 25 percent
are fraudulent.

## FREE PRESS
### Libel

*New York Times, Inc. v. Sullivan*, 376 U.S. 254, 84 S.Ct. 710, 11 L.Ed. 2d 686 (1964)     Held that publications may not be subjected to libel damages for criticism of public officials and their official conduct unless deliberate malice could be shown. *Sullivan* attached stringent conditions to certain kinds of libel actions involving speech attacking public officials. Libel or intentional defamation has not generally been considered a protected expression. A state libel action was brought by a police commissioner in an Alabama court against the *New York Times* for its publication of a paid advertisement which charged police mistreatment of black students protesting racial segregation. It was stipulated that the advertisement contained errors of fact. The trial judge found the statements in the advertisement to be libelous, instructed the jury that injury occurred through publication, and opined that both compensatory and punitive damages could be presumed. Substantial damages were awarded by the jury, which also found malice on the part of the *Times*. The Supreme Court reversed the judgments in a unanimous decision. The Court's position was that libel law must provide free speech safeguards. To allow unrestricted libel actions "would discourage newspapers from carrying 'editorial advertisements' of this type, and so might shut off an important outlet for the promulgation of information and ideas." Such laws would shackle the First Amendment in its attempt to secure protection for the widest possible dissemination of information from diverse and antagonistic sources. Even the factual errors did not jeopardize the advertisement's protected status. The privileged position of the advertisement, clearly "an expression of grievance and protest on one of the major public issues of our time," is not contingent on the truth, popularity, or social utility of the ideas and beliefs which are offered. Mistakes or errors of fact are inevitable in free debate and must be forgiven if freedom of expression is to have the breathing space it needs. Neither does injury to the reputation of a public official itself justify limiting expression. "Criticism of their official conduct does not lose its constitutional protection merely because it is effective criticism and hence diminishes their official reputations." Any rule "compelling the critic of official conduct to guarantee the truth of all his factual assertions—and to do so on pain of libel judgments virtually unlimited in amount—leads to 'self-censorship.'" Such a rule severely dampens the vigor and limits the variety of public debate. The Court did allow for recovery of damages where it can be proved that statements were made with actual malice; that is, with knowledge that it was false or with reckless disregard of whether it was false or not. In concurring opinions, Justices Black and Goldberg argued for the unconditional insulation of the press from libel suits, at least with regard to public officials. *See also* BILL OF RIGHTS, p. 7; FIRST AMENDMENT, p. 77; *HERBERT V. LANDO* (441 U.S. 153: 1979), p. 123.

*Significance*    *New York Times, Inc. v. Sullivan* (376 U.S. 254: 1964) expanded the Court's experience with seditious libel, a special category of libel which involves defamation of the government and its officials. The Alien and Sedition Acts of 1798 would have provided a basic test of seditious libel, but they never reached the Court. The Court has generally included libel in the category of unprotected speech. *Sullivan* provided the Court an opportunity to refine that classification. Libel laws cannot inhibit debate on public issues even if the debate includes strong and unpleasant attacks on the government and its officials. *Sullivan* did hold that public officials could protect themselves through libel actions in situations where false statements were made with reckless disregard of their untruthfulness and with "actual malice." But the *Sullivan* decision approaches an almost unconditional free press position relative to public officials. The Court soon extended *Sullivan* to criminal libel prosecutions in *Garrison v. Louisiana* (379 U.S. 64: 1964). In *Garrison,* the Court said that regardless of limitations in other contexts, "where the criticism is of public officials and their conduct of public business, the interest in private reputation is overborne by the larger public interest, secured by the Constitution in the dissemination of the truth." Yet in *McDonald v. Smith* (86 L.Ed. 2d 384: 1985), the Court held that communications to governmental officials influencing reputation are not immune from libel suits. McDonald had written to President Reagan urging the president not to nominate Smith to the position of United States Attorney. Smith did not receive the nomination and subsequently filed a libel action against McDonald, claiming his letters were malicious and knowingly false. McDonald argued that he was immune from such suit under his First Amendment right to petition the government. In a unanimous decision, the Court said that while the right to petition is guaranteed, "the right to commit libel with impunity is not." The question of whether groups may be protected from defamatory statements was addressed in *Beauharnais v. Illinois* (343 U.S. 250: 1952). In a 5–4 decision, the Court upheld an Illinois statute prohibiting derogatory comment about any racial or religious group. The Court said that "we are precluded from saying that speech concededly punishable when directed at individuals cannot be outlawed if directed at groups with whose position and esteem in society the affiliated individual may be inextricably involved." The dissenters in *Beauharnais* vigorously argued that such a law would greatly inhibit public debate. This view eventually prevailed in *Sullivan* and diminished the current applicability of *Beauharnais*. The Court later reinforced the deliberate malice standard of *Sullivan* in *Bose Corporation v. Consumers Union of the United States, Inc.* (466 U.S. 485: 1984). The Court held that determination of malice in defamation suits is subject to full and thorough review on appeal. *Bose* called for appellate courts to exercise independent judgment and to make their own determination as to whether actual malice had been established with "convincing clarity." This is a more rigorous standard than is normally utilized at appellate levels, and it offers greater protection to publishers defending libel actions by creating a two-tiered system for finding actual malice.

## Editorial Privilege

*Herbert v. Lando*, **441 U.S. 153, 99 S.Ct. 1635, 60 L.Ed. 2d 115 (1979)**    Declared that a plaintiff in a libel action is entitled to inquire into the editorial processes of the defendant. Herbert was a retired Army officer with extended service in Vietnam. He received widespread media attention when he accused his superior officers of covering up reports of atrocities and other war crimes. Herbert conceded his public figure status which required him to demonstrate that the defendants had published a damaging falsehood with actual malice. Some three years after Herbert's disclosures, the Columbia Broadcasting System broadcast a report on Herbert and his charges on the television program "60 Minutes." Lando produced and edited the program. He also published an article on Herbert in the *Atlantic Monthly*. Herbert's suit alleged that the "program and article falsely and maliciously portrayed him as a liar and a person who had made war crime charges to explain his relief from command." In attempting to develop proofs for his case, Herbert tried to obtain the testimony of Lando before trial, but Lando refused, claiming the First Amendment protected against "inquiry into the state of mind of those who edit, produce, or publish, and into the editorial process." The Supreme Court found against Lando in a 6–3 decision. The Court held that the First Amendment does not restrict the sources from which a plaintiff can obtain evidence. Indeed, "it is essential to proving liability that plaintiffs focus on the conduct and state of mind of the defendants." If demonstration of liability is potentially possible, "the thoughts and editorial processes of the alleged defamer would be open to examination." Such examination includes being able to inquire directly from the defendants whether they knew or had reason to suspect that their damaging publication was in error. The editorial privilege sought by Lando would constitute substantial interference with the ability of a defamation plaintiff to establish the ingredients of malice. Further, the outer boundaries sought by Lando are difficult to perceive. In response to the concern that opening the editorial process produced an intolerable chilling effect, the Court suggested that if the claimed inhibition flows from the fear of liability for publishing knowing or reckless falsehoods, those effects are precisely what the *New York Times* and other cases have held to be consistent with the First Amendment. Spreading false information in and of itself carries no First Amendment credentials. If a plaintiff is able to demonstrate liability from direct evidence "which in turn discourages the publication of erroneous information known to be false or probably false, this is no more than what our cases contemplate." Justices Brennan, Stewart, and Marshall dissented, urging at least a partial privilege for the editorial process. *See also* BILL OF RIGHTS, p. 7; FIRST AMENDMENT, p. 77; *NEW YORK TIMES, INC. V. SULLIVAN* (376 U.S. 254: 1964), p. 121.

*Significance*  *Herbert v. Lando* (441 U.S. 153: 1979) established that the editorial practices of a defendant publication could be accessed by a plaintiff in an attempt to show malice. *Sullivan* had set in motion the requirement that malice be demonstrated in libel actions brought by public officials. *Lando* carried the implications of such a demonstration to the point of impinging on freedom of the press by rejecting the notion of editorial privilege. Another issue raised in *Sullivan* relates to the matter of public figures. *Sullivan* protected publications from libel suits where critical comment had been made about governmental officials. Soon thereafter the category of government official was expanded to include public figures, private citizens who are in the midst of public events, or persons who attract wide public attention. In *Rosenbloom v. Metromedia, Inc.* (403 U.S. 29: 1971), the Court went so far as to require reckless falsity in all actions, whether the plaintiff was a public official, a public figure, or a private individual. *Gertz v. Robert Welsh, Inc.* (418 U.S. 323: 1974) held that an individual did not become a public figure simply because the public was interested in a particular event with which that individual was associated. Similarly, a federally funded researcher's media response to receipt of a senator's award for wasting public funds did not give the researchers public figure status in *Hutchinson v. Proxmire* (443 U.S. 111: 1979). Yet another aspect of libel was addressed in 1984. In *Keeton v. Hustler Magazine, Inc.* (465 U.S. 770: 1984) and *Calder v. Jones* (465 U.S. 783: 1984), the Court found that a court in one state had jurisdiction over out-of-state magazines and newspapers if the publications were regularly circulated in that state. Thus plaintiffs are afforded greater discretion in choosing which court will hear their libel actions. The Court maintained that the

First Amendment had no direct bearing on the matter of jurisdiction and that the potential for danger to activities protected by the First Amendment is well integrated into the substantive law governing libel actions. In 1985 the Court added a content criterion for private libel cases in *Dun & Bradstreet, Inc. v. Greenmoss Builders, Inc.* (86 L.Ed. 2d 593: 1985). It ruled that no finding of actual malice need occur unless the case involves a matter of public concern. Greenmoss had sued Dun & Bradstreet for damages based on the circulation of an erroneous credit report. Dun & Bradstreet claimed that Greenmoss must show the erroneous report was published with actual malice. The Court responded that purely private matters are of less First Amendment concern than public matters, thus underscoring the difference between private cases and cases involving public figures. *Greenmoss* increased the likelihood that private parties will collect damages in libel actions by focusing on the element of actual malice. In *Philadelphia Newspapers, Inc. v. Hepps* (89 L.Ed. 2d 783: 1986), however, the Court opined that a private figure suing a newspaper for defamation carries the burden of proving that defamatory statements of public concern are false. Soon after *Hepps*, the Court added the detail in *Anderson v. Liberty Lobby, Inc.* (91 L.Ed. 2d 202: 1986) that trial judges should summarily dismiss, before a trial begins, public figure libel suits unless there is clear and convincing evidence of actual malice. This is the same standard of proof any plaintiff must demonstrate in order to succeed in a libel suit. The ruling enhances the probability that defendants will win pretrial dismissals in libel actions brought by public figures.

## Trial Access

***Richmond Newspapers, Inc. v. Virginia*, 448 U.S. 555, 100 S.Ct. 2814, 75 L.Ed. 2d 973 (1980)**        Determined that the press has a constitutional right of access to criminal trials. In *Richmond Newspapers* the defendant's counsel requested that a murder trial be closed to the public. The prosecutor expressed no objection, and the trial judge ordered the courtroom cleared. Under Virginia law a trial judge has the discretion to exclude from a trial any person whose "presence would impair the conduct of a fair trial." In a 7–1 decision the Supreme Court held the closure order was a violation of the right of access. The Court said this right of the press was protected under the First Amendment. The majority opinion was written by Chief Justice Burger, with Justice Powell not participating in the decision. Chief Justice Burger began with a lengthy treatment of the history of the open trial. This "unbroken, uncontradicted history, supported by reasons as valid today as in centuries past," forced the Court to conclude "that a presumption of openness inheres in the very nature of a criminal trial under our system of justice." The Court majority said the open trial serves a therapeutic purpose for the community, especially in the instance of shocking crimes. Open trials offer protection against abusive or arbitrary behavior. They allow criminal processes "to satisfy the appearance of justice." While access to trials is not specifically provided for in the First Amendment, it is implicit in its guarantees. Without the freedom to attend trials, important aspects of free speech and a free press could be eviscerated. Chief Justice Burger returned to the case at hand in his conclusion. The closure order was defective because the trial judge made no specific finding to support such an order. Alternatives to closure were not explored, there was no recognition of any constitutional right for the press or the public to attend the proceeding, and there was no indication that problems with witnesses could not have been handled otherwise. In a concurring opinion Justice Brennan said that "open trials play a fundamental role in furthering the efforts of any judicial system to assure the criminal defendant a fair and accurate adjudication of guilt or innocence." The open trial is also a means by which a society becomes aware that it is governed equitably. Justice Rehnquist dissented and recast the issue. For him the issue was "whether any provision in the Constitution may fairly be read to prohibit what the trial judge in the Virginia state court system did in this case." Rehnquist would have permitted the trial judge's order to stand. *See also* BRANZBURG V. HAYES (408 U.S. 665: 1972), p. 125; CHANDLER V. FLORIDA (449 U.S. 560: 1981), p. 262; FIRST AMENDMENT, 77; GANNETT COMPANY V. DEPASQUALE (443 U.S. 368: 1979), p. 260; NEBRASKA PRESS ASSOCIATION V. STUART (427 U.S. 530: 1976), p. 259.

*Significance*    *Richmond Newspapers, Inc. v. Virginia* (448 U.S. 555: 1980) clearly distinguished the trial itself from pretrial hearings and elevated the press interest to prevailing weight in the former. In most instances, the Supreme Court has found a criminal defendant to be entitled to insulation from media coverage as a basic requirement of due process in pretrial hearings. Consistent with the objective of minimizing adverse pretrial publicity, the Court allowed closure of pretrial proceedings in *Gannett Company v. DePasquale* (443 U.S. 368: 1979). The Court held in *Nebraska Press Association v. Stuart* (427 U.S. 530: 1976) that material from a public proceeding or record could not be kept from the public through a court gag order. *Nebraska Press Association* also said the press cannot be restrained from reporting what it observes. A balance of press and criminal defendant interests was struck in *Chandler v. Florida* (449 U.S. 560: 1981), in which the Court upheld a policy whereby trials might be broadcast as long as broadcast coverage is not disruptive, intrusive, or prejudicial to the outcome of the trial. In *Press-Enterprise Company v. Superior Court of California I* (464 U.S. 501: 1984), the Court added the detail that the *voir dire* examination must also be open to the public and the press. The presumption of openness can only be overcome by an "overriding interest" which needs protection through narrowly tailored closure. Two years later the Court softened the distinction between trials and pretrial criminal proceedings in *Press-Enterprise Company v. Superior Court of California II* (92 L.Ed. 2d 1: 1986). It more generally narrowed the scope of *Gannett* by saying that closure of pretrial proceedings can only occur where such action is "essential to preserve higher values and is narrowly tailored to serve that interest," a standard which will likely make the closure of pretrial proceedings more difficult.

## Fairness Doctrine

*Red Lion Broadcasting Company v. Federal Communications Commission*, **395 U.S. 367, 89 S.Ct. 1794, 23 L.Ed. 2d 371 (1969)**    Upheld a Federal Communications Commission regulation known as the fairness doctrine. Red Lion broadcast a particular program during which the honesty and character of a third party were impugned. The third party demanded free time for a response, but was refused. The Federal Communications Commission (FCC) then held that Red Lion had failed to satisfy a requirement of equity and equal access. The Supreme Court unanimously upheld the constitutionality of the FCC position. The Court acknowledged that broadcasting is clearly a medium affected by First Amendment interests, but it emphasized some critical differences from the print medium. Among these are the limited number of channels available and the incomparably greater reach of the radio signal. Scarcity of access means Congress "unquestionably has the power to grant and deny licenses," a power vested by Congress in the FCC. The license permits broadcasting, but the licensee "has no constitutional right to be the one who holds the license or to monopolize a radio frequency to the exclusion of his fellow citizens." The Court said the First Amendment does not prevent the government from requiring a licensee to share a frequency with others and to "conduct himself as a proxy or fiduciary" with obligations to present views that are representative of his community and which would otherwise be barred from the airwaves. Government has an obligation to preserve access for divergent views because of the unique character of the broadcast medium. Justice White said the people retain their interest in free speech by radio and have a collective right to the medium functioning consistently with the ends and purposes of the

First Amendment. It is the "right of the viewers and listeners, not the right of broadcasters, which is paramount." Without regulation through the FCC in the form of such rules as the fairness doctrine, station owners and a few networks would have "unfettered power to make time available only to the highest bidders, to communicate only their own views on public issues, people and candidates, and to permit on the air only those with whom they agreed." The Court concluded that there is no sanctuary in the First Amendment for unlimited private censorship operating in a medium not open to all. *See also* BILL OF RIGHTS, p. 7; FIRST AMENDMENT, p. 77; *HERBERT V. LANDO* (440 U.S. 153: 1979), p. 123.

*Significance*     The thrust of *Red Lion Broadcasting Company v. Federal Communications Commission* (395 U.S. 367: 1969) is that a balance must be struck between the First Amendment interests of the broadcast medium and the need to regulate governmentally granted channel monopolies. The fairness doctrine at issue in *Red Lion* had not kept the station from expressing its own views. It had only required that when a station carries a broadcast which attacks an individual personally, reply time be provided. The print media may not be required to do the same thing, however. In *Miami Herald Publishing Company v. Tornillo* (418 U.S. 241: 1974), the Court overturned a Florida right-to-reply statute that required reply space in a newspaper for any political candidate who was attacked. Such required space was found to be as offensive to the First Amendment as prior restraint. This kind of law authorizes governmental "intrusion into the function of editors in choosing what material goes into a newspaper." Similarly, the Court has also held that the airwaves need not become a common carrier with access guaranteed to any private citizen or group. *Columbia Broadcasting System v. Democratic National Committee* (412 U.S. 94: 1973) determined that a broadcaster policy of refusing to sell editorial advertisements was an acceptable practice and not incompatible with the fairness doctrine. The access issue was clouded in 1981 when the Court upheld a right of reasonable access for candidates for federal office in *Columbia Broadcasting System, Inc. v. Federal Communications Commission* (449 U.S. 950: 1981). The power of Congress to prohibit editorials on stations receiving funds from the Corporation for Public Broadcasting was explored in *Federal Communications Commission v. League of Women Voters* (468 U.S. 364: 1984). While broadcasters may be subject to more regulation than other media, the Court said in limiting Congressional power in such cases, that editorial prohibitions affected "precisely that form of speech the framers were most anxious to protect." Content-defined discussion of public issues is the purest example of discourse which must be allowed to proceed unfettered.

## Obscenity Standards

*Miller v. California*, **413 U.S. 15, 93 S.Ct. 2607, 37 L.Ed. 2d 419 (1973)** Tightened definitional standards for obscenity. In *Miller* the Burger Court remodeled and reinterpreted Warren Court obscenity holdings. Miller had been convicted of distributing obscene material. His offense was that he had conducted an aggressive book sales campaign by sending unsolicited brochures through the mail. A five-justice majority upheld Miller's conviction and offered a redefinition of the *Roth* test [*Roth v. United States* (354 U.S. 476: 1957)]. The Court found no fault with *Roth,* but subsequent decisions had "veered sharply away from the *Roth* concept." Thus the need existed to restore its original intent. While many cases had brought about such a need, the major offender was *Fanny Hill,* in which a plurality of the Court produced a "drastically altered test" that required the prosecution to prove a negative. The prosecution had to prove that material was "utterly without redeeming social value—a burden virtually impossible to discharge." (See *Memoirs v. Massachusetts* [383 U.S. 413: 1966], p. 133.) In establishing a revised standard, the Burger Court drew heavily from *Roth.* An obscenity statute must be limited to works which, taken as a whole, appeal to the prurient interest in sex or portray sexual conduct in a patently offensive way. The material when taken as a whole must lack serious literary, artistic, political, or scientific value. The Court specifically rejected the social value test of *Memoirs.* It also proposed some flexibility in applying its guidelines to specific cases. The nation is "simply too big and too diverse" for a uniform standard of prurient interest or patently offensive sexual conduct. The Court viewed it as unrealistic to base proceedings around an abstract formulation. To require a state to try a case around evidence of a national community standard would be an exercise in futility. The Court asserted that people in different states vary in their tastes and attitudes, and "this diversity is not to be strangled by the absolutism of imposed uniformity." State obscenity trials can therefore base evaluation of materials on the contemporary community standards of the particular state. Justices Brennan, Marshall, and Stewart dissented. They argued that obscenity regulations ought to be confined to the distribution of obscene materials to juveniles and unwilling audiences. In his dissent in *Paris Adult Theatre I v. Staton* (413 U.S. 49: 1973), a companion case to *Miller,* Justice Brennan also warned of another expression problem. He said, "The State's interest in regulating morality by suppressing obscenity, while often asserted, remains essentially unfocused and ill-defined." When attempts are made to curtail unprotected speech, protected speech is necessarily involved as well. Thus the effort to serve this speculative interest through regulation of obscene matter "must tread heavily on the rights protected by the First Amendment." Justice Douglas also dissented, offering an absolutist argument for expression in all circumstances. *See also* FIRST AMENDMENT, p. 77; *MEMOIRS V. MASSACHUSETTS* (383 U.S. 413: 1966), p. 133; *ROTH V. UNITED STATES* (354 U.S. 476: 1957), p. 131.

*Significance*　　*Miller v. California* (413 U.S. 15: 1973) represented the first consensus statement on obscenity standards since *Roth* in 1957. *Miller* is of consequence primarily because the Court's rejection of national community standards prompted highly diverse outcomes relative to obscenity regulations. It also removed the social value criterion as an insurmountable obstacle to prosecution. *Miller* provided examples of the kinds of materials that may be offensive enough to be regulated, but a lack of doctrinal clarity remained. Just a year after *Miller,* the Court unanimously reversed an obscenity conviction in *Jenkins v. Georgia* (418 U.S. 153: 1974), overturning a local judgment that the film *Carnal Knowledge* was obscene. The Court cautioned that local juries and their application of community standards are not without First Amendment boundaries. *Miller* did prompt greater regulation, however, and such regulated activities have generally been supported by the Court. In *New York v. Ferber* (458 U.S. 747: 1982), for example, the Court unanimously upheld a statute prohibiting "persons from knowingly promoting a sexual performance by a child under the age of 16." The Court said the states are "entitled to greater leeway in the regulation of pornographic depictions of children." Because state-defined morality "bears so heavily and pervasively on the welfare of children, the balance of compelling interests is clearly struck, and it is permissible to consider these materials as without First Amendment protection." In *Brockett v. Spokane Arcades, Inc.* (86 L.Ed. 2d 394: 1985), however, the Court held that a state obscenity law could not ban lustful material. Just because sexual response is aroused, expression may not therefore be automatically regulated. The Court said that material which does no more than "arouse 'good old-fashioned, healthy' interest in sex" is constitutionally protected.

## Obscenity: Zoning

*Young v. American Mini Theatres, Inc.*, **427 U.S. 50, 96 S.Ct. 2440, 49 L.Ed. 2d 310 (1976)**　　Upheld zoning ordinances regulating locations of adult theaters. *Young* approved amendments to Detroit zoning ordinances providing that adult theaters be licensed. They could not be located within 1,000 feet of any two other "regulated uses" or within 500 feet of any residential area. The other "regulated uses" included some 10 categories of adult entertainment enterprises. An adult theater was defined as one that presented material characterized by emphasis on "specified sexual activities" or "specified anatomical areas." *Young* was a 5–4 decision against several lines of challenge. First, the Court rejected assertions of vagueness in the ordinance because "any element of vagueness in these ordinances has not affected the respondents." The application of the ordinances to the American Mini Theatres "is plain." As for the licensure requirement, the Court noted that the general zoning laws in Detroit imposed requirements on all motion picture theaters. The Court said, "We have no doubt that the municipality may control the location of theaters as well as the location of other commercial establishments." Establishment of such restrictions in themselves is not prohibited as prior restraint. The "mere fact that the commercial exploitation of material protected by the First Amendment is subject to zoning and other licensing requirements is not sufficient reason for invalidating these ordinances." The Court also considered whether the 1,000 foot restriction constituted an improper content-based classification. The Court said that "even within the area of protected speech, a difference in content may require a different governmental response." Citing the public figure category in libel law and prohibitions on exhibition of obscenity to juveniles and unconsenting adults, the Court held that the First Amendment did not foreclose content distinctions. They "rest squarely on an appraisal of the content of the material otherwise within a constitutionally protected area." Even though the First Amendment does not allow total suppression, the Court held that a state may legitimately use the content of mini theater materials as the basis for placing them in a different classification from other motion pictures. Finally, the Court upheld the regulated use classification on the basis of the city's interest in preserving the character of its neighborhoods. Detroit has a legitimate interest in attempting to preserve the quality of urban life. It is an interest which "must be accorded high respect," and the city must be allowed "a reasonable opportunity to experiment with solutions to an admittedly serious problem." Justices Brennan, Stewart, Marshall, and Blackmun dissented, basing their opinion on the vagueness and content orientation of the ordinance. *See also* BILL OF RIGHTS, p. 7; FIRST AMENDMENT, p. 77; *MILLER V. CALIFORNIA* (413 U.S. 15: 1973), p. 134.

*Significance*     *Young v. American Mini Theatres, Inc.* (427 U.S. 50: 1976) represents a new wave of cases raising issues about local regulation of "adult entertainment." The Court has generally supported local regulation provided expression is not completely prohibited and a compelling interest can be demonstrated. Meeting these conditions is not always easy, however. In *Erznoznick v. Jacksonville* (422 U.S. 205: 1975), the Court struck down an ordinance which prohibited the exhibition of films containing nudity if the screen could be seen from a public street. The Court cited the limited privacy interest of persons on the streets, but it also stressed the overly broad sweep of the ordinance. In *Schad v. Borough of Mount Ephraim* (452 U.S. 61: 1981), the Court invalidated a zoning ordinance which banned live entertainment in a borough establishment. Convictions under the ordinance had been secured against an adult bookstore operator for having live nude dancers performing in the establishment. The borough argued that permitting such entertainment would conflict with its plan to create a commercial area catering only to the immediate needs of residents. The Court considered such justification "patently insufficient." The ordinance prohibited a "wide range of expression that has long been held to be within the protection of the First and Fourteenth Amendments." Ten years after *Young*, the Court once again reviewed a local attempt to regulate the location of adult theaters in *City of Renton v. Playtime Theatres, Inc.* (89 L.Ed. 2d 29: 1986). Using the same rationale stated in *Young*, the Court upheld a municipality's authority to require dispersal of such establishments. Since the municipal ordinance did not bar adult theaters entirely, it was reviewed as a time, place, and manner regulation. Such regulations are acceptable as long as they serve a substantial interest and do not unreasonably limit avenues of communication. Justice Rehnquist said for the Court that the First Amendment requires only that a local unit refrain from denying individuals a "reasonable opportunity to open and operate an adult theater within the city." He said the city of Renton easily met that requirement in the ordinance under review.

## Film Licensure

*Freedman v. Maryland*, **380 U.S. 51, 85 S.Ct. 734, 13 L.Ed. 2d 649 (1965)** Upheld a film licensure requirement with particular procedural safeguards. *Freedman* explores the fact that most cases challenging obscenity enactments focus on the substantive distinction between protected and unprotected expression. The problem is defining obscenity. *Freedman* targeted the actual technique of censorship. Freedman violated a Maryland statute requiring licensure to exhibit motion pictures. He refused to submit a film to the State Board of Censors prior to showing it. Maryland stipulated that the film would have been licensed had it been submitted. Freedman sought, however, to have movie censorship declared unconstitutional per se. The Court did not go as far as Freedman wanted, but it unanimously reversed his conviction. The Court said a prior restraint mechanism bears a "heavy presumption against its constitutional validity." Specifically, the "administration of a censorship proceeding puts the initial burden on the exhibitor or distributor." The justices went on to outline procedural safeguards "designed to obviate the dangers of the censorship system." First, the "burden of proving that the film is unprotected expression must rest with the censor." Second, while advance submissions may be required, no film may be banned through means "which would lend an effect of finality to the censor's determination." Third, a film cannot be banned unless the process permits judicial determination of the restraint. Fourth, various steps in the process must not take too long. "The exhibitor must be assured that the censor will within a specified brief period, either issue a license or go to court to restrain the showing of the film." Any restraints imposed prior to final judicial determination must be "limited to preservation of the status quo for the shortest fixed period." Finally, the "procedure must also assure a prompt final judicial decision, to minimize the deterrent effect of an interim and possibly erroneous denial of a license." These safeguards are absolute requirements. Without such limitations, "it may prove too burdensome to seek review of the censor's determination." The Court concluded that the Maryland censorship process did not sufficiently incorporate the stipulated safeguards. *See also* BILL OF RIGHTS, p. 7; FIRST AMENDMENT, p. 77; *KINGSLEY BOOKS, INC. V. BROWN* (354 U.S. 436: 1957), p. 139.

*Significance*     *Freedman v. Maryland* (380 U.S. 51: 1965) raised serious prior restraint questions. Censorship of films occurred from the time films were first produced, and Supreme Court decisions extended virtually no free press protections for them. As motion pictures evolved, however, their unprotected status changed and censorship techniques such as those in *Freedman* demanded Court attention. A key case in elevating films to partial coverage by the First Amendment was *Burstyn v. Wilson* (343 U.S. 495: 1952). The Court found that it "cannot be doubted that motion pictures are a significant medium for the communication of ideas." Although films may possess a "greater capacity for evil," such potential "does not authorize substantially unbridled censorship." While *Freedman* did not condemn the practice of censorship per se, it established important procedural requirements. Arbitrary interference with exhibitors is not permitted. In *Roaden v. Kentucky* (413 U.S. 496: 1973), the Court unanimously determined that a warrantless seizure of a film during its showing by a county sheriff was a prior restraint. Similarly, in *Southeastern Promotions, Ltd. v. Conrad* (419 U.S. 892: 1975), the Court held that a city's refusal to rent a city facility for a performance of *Hair* was a prior restraint. The Court said city officials may deny a forum to an obscene production, but such a decision must be made through a properly safeguarded process. In *Heller v. New York* (413 U.S. 483: 1973) the Court did uphold the seizure of a film under authority of a warrant from a judge who had viewed it prior to signing the warrant. Finally, in *New York v. P. J. Video, Inc.* (89 L.Ed. 2d 871: 1986), the Court reviewed a lower court ruling that established a higher probable cause standard for issuing warrants to seize suspect books or films as opposed to other contraband such as weapons. In a 6–3 decision, the Burger Court ruled that the First Amendment required no higher standard. Such warrant applications should be reviewed with the same standards used for warrant applications generally: that there is a fair probability evidence of a crime will be found in the location to be searched.

## ASSEMBLY AND PROTEST
### Public Premises

*Adderley v. Florida*, **385 U.S. 39, 87 S.Ct. 242, 17 L.Ed. 2d 149 (1966)**    Held that demonstrators may be barred from assembly on the grounds of a county jail. *Adderley* considered whether certain locations might be put off-limits to demonstrations or assemblies. Adderley and a number of others were convicted of trespass for gathering at a county jail to protest the arrest of several students the day before, as well as local policies of racial segregation at the jail itself. When the demonstrators would not leave the jail grounds when asked, they were warned of possible arrest for trespass. Adderley and others remained on the premises, were arrested, and were subsequently tried and convicted. The Court upheld the convictions in a 5–4 decision. The Court focused on the question of whether the trespass convictions deprived the demonstrators of their freedom of speech. Through Justice Black, the Court majority concluded that "nothing in the Constitution of the United States prevented Florida from even-handed enforcement of its general trespass statute against those refusing to obey the sheriff's order to remove themselves from what amounted to the curtilage of the jailhouse." The fact that the jail was a public building did not automatically entitle the protesters to demonstrate there. The state, no less than a private owner of property, has power to preserve the property under its control for the use to which it is lawfully dedicated. The security purpose for which the jail was dedicated outweighed the expression interests of the protesters. The justices felt that to find for Adderley would be to endorse "the assumption that people who want to propagandize protests or views have a constitutional right to do so whenever and wherever they please." The Court categorically rejected that premise and concluded its opinion by saying the Constitution does not forbid a state to control the use of its own property for its own lawful nondiscriminatory purposes. Justice Douglas dissented, joined by Chief Justice Warren and Justices Brennan and Fortas. Justice Douglas considered the jailhouse "one of the seats of government" and an "obvious center for protest." *See also* FIRST AMENDMENT, p. 77; *PRUNEYARD SHOPPING CENTER V. ROBINS* (447 U.S. 74: 1980), p. 144; *TINKER V. DES MOINES SCHOOL DISTRICT* (393 U.S. 503: 1969), p. 113.

*Significance*     *Adderley v. Florida* (385 U.S. 39: 1966) illustrated the "speech plus" test. In certain situations speech is defined as conduct beyond oral expression itself. The additional conduct is subject to regulation at a cost to expression. In *Cox v. Louisiana* (379 U.S. 536: 1965), the Court upheld a state statute that prohibited picketing near a courthouse. It said a state could legitimately insulate its judicial proceedings from demonstrations. While restrictions were said to be warranted in *Adderley* and *Cox,* breach of the peace convictions of persons demonstrating on the grounds of a state capitol were reversed in *Edwards v. South Carolina* (372 U.S. 229: 1963). Similarly, a peaceful sit-in at a public library was protected in *Brown v. Louisiana* (383 U.S. 131: 1966). More recently, the Court struck down an ordinance which prohibited picketing in the proximity of school buildings when classes were in session in *Chicago Police Department v. Mosley* (408 U.S. 92: 1972). The ordinance was invalidated largely because it excepted labor picketing from the ban. The Court did suggest the city had a legitimate interest in preventing school disruption, however. Time, place, and manner restrictions have generally been recognized by the Court, provided that significant governmental interests can be demonstrated. Trespass on private property was subject to punishment for many years, although civil rights sit-ins forced a legislative reevaluation of that policy. The Supreme Court successfully avoided dealing with the sit-in issue directly until passage of the Civil Rights Act of 1964. The Act prohibited the discriminatory practices in public accommodations that had triggered the sit-in demonstrations in the first place. In a case involving another use of public property, the Court held in *City Council of Los Angeles v. Taxpayers for Vincent* (466 U.S. 789: 1984) that a municipality could ban the posting of political campaign signs on utility poles. The ban was seen to be content neutral and directed toward a legitimate aesthetic interest. The purpose of the regulation was "unrelated to the suppression of ideas," and interfered with expression only to the extent necessary to eliminate visual clutter. The Court noted that the ban on posting signs did not impinge on any alternative modes of communication.

# ASSOCIATION
## Electoral Process

***Buckley v. Valeo*, 424 U.S. 1, 96 S.Ct. 612, 46 L.Ed. 2d 659 (1976)** Examined the constitutionality of the Federal Election Campaign Act of 1974. *Buckley* considered the act against various First Amendment challenges, including the possibility that regulation of the electoral process impinges upon individual and group expression. The Federal Election Campaign Act was passed in the wake of Watergate. It sought to protect the electoral process by (1) limiting political campaign contributions; (2) establishing ceilings on several categories of campaign expenditures; (3) requiring extensive and regular disclosure of campaign contributors and expenditures; (4) providing public financing for presidential campaigns; and (5) creating a Federal Election Commission to administer the act. Suit was filed by a diverse collection of individuals and groups, which included United States Senator James Buckley, the Eugene McCarthy presidential campaign, the Libertarian Party, the American Conservative Union, and the New York Civil Liberties Union. By differing majorities, the Court upheld those portions of the act which provided for campaign contribution limits, disclosure, public financing, and the Election Commission. The section imposing limits on expenditures was invalidated. In a *per curiam* opinion, the Court said the act's contribution and expenditure ceiling "reduces the quantity of expression because virtually every means of communicating ideas in today's society requires the expenditure of money." The Court distinguished, however, between limits on contributions and limits on those things for which the contributions might be spent. While the latter represents substantial restraint on the quantity and diversity of political speech, limits on contributions involve "little direct restraint." The contributor's freedom to discuss candidates and issues is not infringed in any way. Even though contributions may underwrite some costs of conveying a campaign's views, the contributions must be transformed into political expression by persons other than the contributor. The Court acknowledged a legitimate governmental interest in protecting the "integrity of our system of representative democracy" from quid pro quo arrangements that might arise from financial contributions. Expenditure limits, on the other hand, severely burden one's ability to speak one's mind and engage in vigorous advocacy. Neither is the First Amendment to be used to equalize political influence. "The concept that government may restrict the speech of some elements of our society in order to enhance the relative voice of others is wholly foreign to the First Amendment." By striking the expenditure limits, the Court allowed unlimited use of personal wealth or expenditures made on behalf of campaigns separate from the actual campaign organization of a candidate. On the matter of disclosure, the Court agreed that the requirement might deter some contributions but viewed it as a "least restrictive means of curbing the evils of campaign ignorance and corruption." The Court also upheld the act's public financing provisions by rejecting a claim that a differential funding formula for major and minor parties was unconstitutional. *See also* FIRST AMENDMENT, p. 77; *NAACP V. ALABAMA* (357 U.S. 449: 1958), p. 147; *WHITNEY V. CALIFORNIA* (274 U.S. 357: 1927), p. 149

*Significance*        *Buckley v. Valeo* (424 U.S. 1: 1976) generated important followup questions regarding regulation of the electoral process. In *First National Bank of Boston v. Bellotti* (435 U.S. 765: 1978), the Court struck down a state statute prohibiting the use of corporate funds for the purpose of influencing a referendum question. Without a showing that the corporation's advocacy "threatened imminently to undermine democratic processes," the state has no interest sufficient to limit a corporation's expression of views on a public issue. In *Consolidated Edison Company v. Public Service Commission of New York* (447 U.S. 530: 1980), the Court overturned a state commission order prohibiting utilities from enclosing inserts discussing public policy issues in billing envelopes. The Court said the order was aimed at the pronuclear energy content of the insert and was not justifiable as a time, place, or manner restriction on speech. Neither may corporations be forced to disseminate messages with which they disagree. In *Pacific Gas and Electric Company v. Public Utilities Commission* (89 L.Ed. 2d 1: 1986), the Court ruled that a state regulatory agency could not order a privately owned utility to send inserts from a consumer group in their quarterly billing envelopes. The Court said freedom of speech "includes within it the choice of what not to say." The Court added that such freedom of choice is not dependent on whether the protection is sought by an individual or a corporation. In *Citizens Against Rent Control/Coalition for Fair Housing v. City of Berkeley* (450 U.S. 908: 1981), the Court struck down a municipal ordinance limiting contributions to organizations formed to support or oppose ballot issues. With only Justice White dissenting, the Court drew heavily on Buckley and concluded that the ordinance went too far in restraining individual and associational rights of expression. The Court extended the *Buckley* reasoning in *Federal Election Commission v. National Conservative Political Action Committee* (470 U.S. 480: 1985), saying the Federal Election Campaign Act could not limit political action committees to an expenditure of $1,000 for promoting the candidacies of publicly funded presidential aspirants. Such an expenditure limit impermissibly infringed on First Amendment speech and association rights.

# 2. The Fourth Amendment

## Informants and Probable Cause

*Massachusetts v. Upton*, **466 U.S. 727, 104 S.Ct. 2085, 80 L.Ed. 2d 721 (1984)**    Held that the totality of circumstances standard is appropriate in determining probable cause for a warrant based on information provided by an informant. *Massachusetts v. Upton* represents the Burger Court's reformulation of policy relative to the use of informant information in the warrant process. Upton was convicted of several offenses in a trial where evidence obtained through a search based on informant information was admitted. The Massachusetts Supreme Court reversed Upton's conviction, ruling that the affidavit supporting the warrant authorizing the search was defective. The affidavit did not establish probable cause based on the two-pronged test established in *Aguilar v. Texas* (378 U.S. 108: 1964). Massachusetts appealed, and the United States Supreme Court reversed the state supreme court in a 7–2 decision. Through a *per curiam* opinion, the Court said the probable cause requirement could be adequately maintained through a "totality of circumstances" approach. The two-pronged test required that affidavits submitted in support of warrants establish the means by which the informant came to know the information given to authorities—the so-called "basis of knowledge" prong. The second requirement stipulated that the affidavit must establish either the general veracity of the informant or the specific reliability of his or her information in the instant case. The Court chose to move away from both requirements in *Upton,* with the language of the decision making the Court's new position unmistakably clear. The Court said it now rejected the two-pronged test as "hypertechnical" and "divorced from the 'factual and practical considerations of everyday life on which reasonable and prudent men, not legal technicians, act.'" The Court said it is "wiser" to abandon the two-pronged test and replace it with a totality of circumstances approach which is more in keeping with the practical, commonsense decisions demanded of magistrates granting warrants. The totality analysis permits necessary flexibility rather than encouraging "an excessively technical dissection" of informant tips. The previous standard allowed undue attention to isolated issues. The new approach is a "more deferential standard of review," which permits the magistrate to put together pieces of evidence in a more general way to support his or her decision to issue a warrant. Justices Brennan and Marshall dissented. In the related case of *Illinois v. Gates* (462 U.S. 213: 1983), they expressed a preference for retaining the two-pronged test. *See also* DRAPER V. UNITED STATES (358 U.S. 307: 1959), p. 160; FOURTH AMENDMENT, p. 159; INFORMANT, p. 426; PROBABLE CAUSE, p. 446.

*Significance*    *Massachusetts v. Upton* (466 U.S. 727: 1984) represents the abandonment of the Court's stricter standards regarding informant information existing since the mid-1960s. *Aguilar v. Texas* had established two key criteria. First, supporting information must be provided that speaks to the reliability and trustworthiness of the informant, a special problem when the informant is unnamed or anonymous. Second, the substance of the informant's information must be supported by other evidence. In *United States v. Spinelli* (393 U.S. 410: 1969), the Court reversed a conviction because insufficient support had been provided for a tip from an anonymous informant. The Court said the identity of an informant was clearly a factor in assessing his or her credibility. If the identity is either withheld or unknown, *Spinelli* required additional support to compensate for the informant's anonymity. *Spinelli* also demanded the full development of the basis upon which the informant concluded that criminal conduct had occurred. In *United States v. Harris* (403 U.S. 573: 1971), the Court said that hearsay may be used when seeking a warrant, thus modifying *Spinelli* by holding that information about the reputation of the person to be searched could be used to support the warrant request. Further, *Harris* held that the previous receipt of reliable information was not required to demonstrate an informant's reliability. *Harris* reinterpreted both *Aguilar* and *Spinelli* by assigning weight to a suspect's reputation and by deferring to the experience and knowledge of police officers in assessing the credibility of information from informants. The modification of *Aguilar* and *Spinelli* standards was continued in *Illinois v. Gates*, where the Court rejected the two-pronged test for the first time. The *Aguilar* and *Spinelli* elements of informant veracity, reliability, and basis of knowledge remain considerations for magistrates issuing warrants, but the totality of circumstances approach of *Gates* and *Upton* is said by the Court to be more flexible and "will better achieve the accommodation of public and private interests that the Fourth Amendment requires." The impact of this adjustment will have to be measured over time. What is certain is that *Gates* and *Upton* constitute a major policy shift in the Court's interpretation of what it means to be secure against unreasonable searches and seizures.

## Good Faith Exception

*United States v. Leon*, **468 U.S. 897, 104 S.Ct. 3405, 82 L.Ed. 2d 677 (1984)**    Upheld a "good faith" exception to the exclusionary rule. *United States v. Leon* involved an attempt to suppress evidence obtained through a search conducted under warrant. It was determined that the affidavit supporting the application for a warrant did not actually establish probable cause. The lower courts ruled that despite the fact that police officers acted in good faith and pursuant to what they felt was a legally sufficient warrant, the evidence had to be suppressed. In a 6–3 decision, the Supreme Court reversed. The opinion of the Court was written by Justice White, who defined the issue in *Leon* as whether the exclusionary rule should be modified to allow admission of evidence seized "in reasonable, good faith reliance" on a search warrant that is subsequently held to be defective. White commented on the exclusionary rule itself, saying there is no provision in the Fourth Amendment "expressly precluding the use of evidence obtained in violation of its commands." The exclusionary rule operates as a judicially created remedy designed to protect Fourth Amendment rights generally rather than as a "personal constitutional right of the person aggrieved." White pointed to the "substantial social cost" exacted by the rule, and he argued that unbending application of it "impedes the truth-finding functions of judge and jury." An objectionable collateral consequence is that some guilty defendants go free or receive reduced sentences through plea bargaining. Indiscriminate application of the rule also generates disrespect for the law and the administration of justice. This is more likely when law enforcement officers have acted in good faith or their transgressions have been minor. For these reasons, recent Court decisions have focused on the remedial objectives of the rule, and the Court has become more inclined to adopt a balancing approach. White said that application of the rule must continue where a Fourth Amendment violation is substantial and deliberate, but the rule should be modified to allow use of evidence obtained by officers reasonably relying on a warrant. The courts must be sure that affidavits supporting the warrant are not knowingly or recklessly false, and that the magistrate issuing the warrant has functioned in a neutral and detached manner. To extend the rule further serves no deterrent function. The rule is designed to limit police misconduct rather than punish errors of judges and magistrates. It is contrary to the rule's purpose to apply it to diminish objectively reasonable police conduct. Once the warrant has been issued, there is "literally nothing more the policeman can do in seeking to comply with the law." Penalizing the officer for a magistrate's error rather than his own "cannot logically contribute to the deterrence of Fourth Amendment violations." In the case of *Leon*, since the reliance of officers on the judge's determination was objectively reasonable, the exclusion of evidence based on their activity was not necessary. Justices Brennan, Marshall, and Stevens dissented. Brennan called the decision one of a series aimed at the "gradual but determined strangulation of the exclusionary rule." Brennan felt the Court ignored the fundamental constitutional importance of what was at stake in *Leon*. He said fighting crime will always be a sufficiently critical and pressing concern to present "temptations of expediency" leading to "forsaking our commitment to the protection of individual liberty and privacy." Stevens said the Court should not so easily concede the existence of a constitutional violation for which there is no remedy. He said to do so is to convert the Bill of Rights into an unenforceable honor code that the police may follow at their discretion. See also EXCLUSIONARY RULE, p. 409; FOURTH AMENDMENT, p. 159; *MAPP V. OHIO* (367 U.S. 643: 1961), p. 172; *STONE V. POWELL* (428 U.S. 465: 1976), p. 173.

*Significance*        The Court said in *United States v. Leon* (454 U.S. 869: 1984) that the exclusionary rule may be modified to permit use of evidence seized by police officers as long as they reasonably relied on a warrant subsequently found to be defective. *Leon* represents a substantial alteration of the exclusionary rule, but the Court was careful to point out that the "good faith" exception does not apply under all conditions. The police may not mislead a magistrate or knowingly offer false information in support of an affidavit, for example. Neither may police officers claim good faith when it is clear the magistrate is not neutral. Further, reasonable reliance on a warrant cannot exist where it lacks specificity or is otherwise facially defective. In the related case of *Immigration and Naturalization Service v. Delgado* (466 U.S. 210: 1984), the Court upheld use of factory sweeps as a means of apprehending illegal aliens. The practice involved entry into a workplace without advance notice to question employees about the status of their citizenship. The Court did not see this practice as a seizure and ruled that no warrant was required. In *Oliver v. United States* and *Maine v. Thornton* (466 U.S. 170: 1984), the Court said that police officers do not need a warrant to search for drugs in open fields. An open field was not found to be a person, house, or effect entitled to Fourth Amendment protection. It possessed no expectation of privacy. Similarly the Court upheld warrantless aerial observation and aerial photography in two cases decided in 1986. In *California v. Ciraolo* (90 L.Ed. 2d 210: 1986), the Court permitted aerial surveillance of a fenced private backyard. The police suspected that marijuana was being grown on the property. In a 5–4 decision, the Court said any citizen flying in the airspace over the yard could have seen what a police officer observed. The Fourth

Amendment does not require that police officers flying in public airspace must obtain a warrant to observe what is visible to the naked eye. In *Dow Chemical Company v. United States* (90 L.Ed. 2d 226: 1986), the Court permitted the Environmental Protection Agency (EPA) to use aerial photographic equipment for measuring emissions at Dow's production facilities to determine whether Dow was in compliance with Clean Air Act standards. The Court said that open areas of an industrial complex are comparable to open fields for which persons cannot demand privacy. In *Thompson v. Louisiana* (469 U.S. 17: 1984), the Court opined that a search was not entitled to a warrant exception simply because it occurred at a murder scene. Thus the Court's general opinion in recent years does not appear to support claims of Fourth Amendment violations. An interesting good faith immunity issue was raised in *Malley v. Briggs* (89 L.Ed. 2d 271: 1986). On the basis of approved telephone monitoring, Officer Malley prepared felony complaints against the Briggs. Malley presented arrest warrants to a judge who signed them. The Briggs were subsequently arrested, but a grand jury failed to find cause to indict them. They then brought a damage action against Malley under 42 United States Code Section 1983, claiming Malley violated their rights by applying for the warrants. Malley in turn claimed absolute immunity from such a suit. The Court held that Malley was entitled only to limited immunity from damage liability. Such cases must be judged by the objective reasonableness standard which provides "ample protection to all but the plainly incompetent or those who knowingly violate the law." In another 42 United States Code Section 1983 decision, the Court held in *City of Los Angeles v. Heller* (89 L.Ed. 2d 806: 1986) that if a jury finds an arrest was made with probable cause and without unreasonable force, the absence of constitutional injury precludes any damage award against a municipality based on the actions of the arresting officer.

## Warrantless Arrest

*Welsh v. Wisconsin*, **466 U.S. 740, 104 S.Ct. 2091, 80 L.Ed. 2d 732 (1984)**     Held that police officers may not enter a person's home at night without a warrant to make an arrest for a nonjailable traffic violation unless there are exigent circumstances. *Welsh v. Wisconsin* involved an erratic driving incident reported to authorities by a witness. The driver abandoned the car, but officers learned of his address by checking the registration. Without a warrant, they went to Welsh's residence, entered, and found him in bed. He was arrested and taken to police headquarters, where he refused to take a breath test. The trial court ruled his arrest to be lawful and suspended his license for failure to take the test. The Wisconsin Supreme Court upheld the arrest. The Supreme Court reversed the state court in a 6–3 decision. The opinion of the Court was delivered by Justice Brennan. In 1980, the Court held in *Payton v. New York* (445 U.S. 573: 1980) that a warrantless arrest in a person's home was prohibited unless both probable cause and exigent circumstances existed. *Welsh* examined one aspect of the question of what constitutes exigent circumstances. Brennan said it is axiomatic that "the physical entry of the home is the chief evil against which the wording of the Fourth Amendment is directed." Accordingly, warrantless searches and arrests that occur inside a home are presumptively unreasonable, and exceptions are few and carefully delineated. The police bear a heavy burden when attempting to demonstrate an urgent need that might justify a warrantless search or arrest. Brennan said the Court's hesitation in finding exigencies is especially appropriate where the offense for which there is probable cause to arrest is relatively minor. When the government's interest is only to arrest for such an offense, the presumption of unreasonableness is difficult to rebut. Futhermore, the government usually should be able to make such arrests only with a warrant issued by a neutral and detached magistrate. When an officer undertakes to act as his own magistrate, he or she ought to be able to point to some real, immediate, and serious consequence if seeking the warrant is postponed. The nature of the underlying offense is an important factor in the exigent circumstances calculus. Most courts have refused to permit warrantless home arrests for nonfelonious crimes. The warrant exception for exigent circumstances is narrowly drawn to cover real and uncontrived emergencies. The exception is thus limited to the investigation of serious crimes. Misdemeanors are excluded. It is difficult to conceive of a warrantless home arrest that would not be unreasonable when the underlying offense is minor. In this case, the only potential emergency claimed was the need to ascertain the petitioner's blood-alcohol level. The state's classification of the first offense for driving while intoxicated as a noncriminal, civil forfeiture offense is the best indication of the state's interest in precipitating an arrest. Given this expression of the state's interest, a warrantless home arrest cannot be upheld simply because evidence of the petitioner's blood-alcohol level might have dissipated while the police obtained a warrant. Justices White and Rehnquist dissented, feeling the state had a substantial enough interest to justify a warrantless, exigent circumstance search, despite the noncriminal classification. They saw the need to prevent the deterioration of evidence as an exigent circumstance. Chief Justice Burger said he would have preferred to examine the questions presented by the dissenters in a "more appropriate case." *See also* EXIGENT CIRCUMSTANCE, p. 410; FOURTH AMENDMENT, p. 159; PROBABLE CAUSE, p. 446.

*Significance*   The Court established in *Welsh v. Wisconsin* (466 U.S. 740: 1984) that a warrantless entry of a house to make an arrest for a civil traffic offense was prohibited by the Fourth Amendment unless exigent circumstances existed. The matter of how much authority officials possess to enter private homes to make a warrantless arrest has always been troublesome. In *Payton v. New York* (445 U.S. 573: 1980), the Court said that the authority to enter a private residence without a warrant was absolutely contingent on the presence of probable cause and an emergency. In *Payton,* the police were attempting to make a routine arrest for a felony level offense, but the Court held that the arrest was unreasonable. *Payton* did not attempt to define what constituted a sufficiently exigent circumstance to support a warrantless arrest, however. The pursuit of a fleeing suspect into a private residence was permissible, but beyond that the contours of judicial policy remained vague. *Welsh* thus attempted to clarify the nature of an emergency. The Court insisted that the state show an urgent need for a warrantless arrest, suggesting that demonstration of an actual exigency may be virtually impossible if the underlying offense is minor. If a state has classified an offense as minor, not even the preservation of evidence produces a sufficiently compelling need for a warrantless arrest.

## Warrantless Search

*Michigan v. Tyler,* **436 U.S. 499, 98 S.Ct. 1942, 56 L.Ed. 2d 486 (1978)**   A consideration of the concept of exigent circumstance as an exception to the search warrant requirement. A fire began about midnight in a store co-owned by Tyler. Before the fire was fully extinguished, the fire chief made a cursory inspection of the fire scene. Among the things noted at the time were containers of flammable liquid. The police were immediately informed and a fuller investigation commenced. After leaving the scene for several hours, both police and fire officials returned to the unsecured location around 8 A.M., examined the scene more systematically, and seized evidence. In the days which followed, additional visits to the scene were made and additional evidence, largely in the form of photographs, was obtained. None of the inspections, either those taking place during the fire itself or those occurring up to thirty days after the fire, was conducted with a warrant or with Tyler's consent. The Supreme Court, with Justice Brennan not participating, unanimously ruled that the searches occurring during and immediately after the fire had satisfied the conditions of the exigent exception. Those occurring more than nine hours after the fire did not satisfy the exigent circumstance conditions. The majority rejected the argument that no privacy interests remained, the badly burned premises had been abandoned, and that searches by officials other than police are not encompassed by the Fourth Amendment. Warrants are generally required, and an official must show more than "the bare fact that a fire has occurred." Even though there is a "vital social objective in ascertaining the cause of the fire, the magistrate can perform the important function of preventing harassment by keeping that invasion to a minimum." However, this search was subject to the exigent circumstance exception. The Court said, "A burning building clearly presents an exigency of sufficient proportions to render a warrantless entry 'reasonable.'" The authorities were properly on the premises, and could thus seize evidence in plain view. Justice Stewart argued that "it would defy reason to suppose that a fireman must secure a warrant or consent before entering a burning structure to put out the blaze. And once in the building for this purpose, firefighters may seize evidence of arson that is in plain view." Justices Marshall and White would have restricted the warrantless search up to the point the fire was extinguished. They would have required a warrant for the return inspection the morning after the fire. Justice Rehnquist considered the search of a "routine and regulatory" nature and would have placed it outside the conventional Fourth Amendment coverage. *See also* FOURTH AMENDMENT, p. 159; *UNITED STATES V. EDWARDS* (415 U.S. 800: 1974), p. 176.

*Significance*     Warrantless searches are permitted if exigent or emergency circumstances can be demonstrated. *Michigan v. Tyler* (436 U.S. 499: 1978) examined the exigent circumstance exception associated with entry into burning property. The exigent circumstance exception is based upon the recognition that prior authorization through a warrant may simply be impossible under the conditions. To expect an officer to interrupt the "hot pursuit" of a suspect to obtain a warrant to continue the chase onto private property is generally regarded as unreasonable. Key to proceeding without a warrant is demonstrating a compelling emergency. In *Tyler*, the Court found the presence of firefighters on the burning private property to be justified. Once legally on the property, the officers could reasonably investigate the origin of the fire. The investigation was permitted because it could be related not only to the preservation of potential evidence of crime, but also because it was necessary to reduce the likelihood of the fire recurring. Thus the fire was viewed as an emergency sufficient to allow the fire officials to be on the premises legally. Their legal presence also allowed warrantless investigation for a reasonable time following the onset of the fire. Those searches that occurred in the days following the fire were not seen as contemporaneous with the exigency which permitted the initial legal entry onto the property. Once property can be secured, the exigency ends and no necessity for proceeding without a warrant remains. In a more recent arson search case, *Michigan v. Clifford* (464 U.S. 287: 1984), the Court held that where "expectations of privacy" remain for fire-damaged premises, administrative warrants are required for searches intended to determine the cause and place of origin of the fire. Privacy expectations are "especially strong" for a private home, and a delay between the fire and the search brings with it warrant requirements. Once the cause and place of origin of the fire have been determined, the scope of the search is limited, and the search for additional evidence of criminal conduct can proceed only under a search warrant obtained on a showing of probable cause.

## Warrantless Search

*Washington v. Chrisman,* 455 U.S. 1, 102 S.Ct. 812, 70 L.Ed. 2d 778 (1982)    Involved a plain view seizure of evidence located in a residence some distance from the place of a legitimate arrest. Chrisman was stopped by a campus police officer for illegally possessing liquor. The officer asked Chrisman for identification. Chrisman had no identification on him and requested that he be permitted to return to his dormitory room to obtain it. The officer agreed and accompanied him to the residence hall. The officer stood at the open door of Chrisman's room and watched him look for identification. While waiting, the officer noticed what he believed to be marijuana lying "in plain view" on a desk in the room. The officer entered the room, confirmed that the substance was marijuana, and advised Chrisman and his roommate of their rights. The students consented to a broader search of the room which yielded more marijuana and LSD. The students subsequently sought to have the evidence suppressed on the ground that the officer was not entitled to enter the room and either examine or seize the marijuana and LSD without a warrant. In a 6–3 decision, the Supreme Court upheld the search. The plain view doctrine was critical for the majority. The doctrine "permits a law enforcement officer to seize what clearly is incriminating evidence or contraband when it is discovered in a place where the officer has a right to be." The majority concluded that the officer had properly accompanied Chrisman to his room, and that remaining at the doorway was irrelevant to sustaining the warrantless search. The officer had "an unimpeded view of and access to the area's contents and its occupants." The officer's "right to custodial control did not evaporate with his choice to hesitate briefly in the doorway." He had a "right to act as soon as he observed the seeds and the pipe. This is a classic instance of incriminating evidence found in plain view when a police officer, for unrelated but entirely legitimate reasons, obtains lawful access to an individual's area of privacy." Justices Brennan, Marshall, and White dissented, saying the plain view doctrine "does not authorize an officer to enter a dwelling without a warrant to seize contraband merely because the contraband is visible from outside the dwelling." For them, the failure of the officer to enter the room with Chrisman was a fatal defect. Further, the exigency of custody pursuant to arrest did not justify, in the officer's mind, entry into the room. *See also* COOLIDGE V. NEW HAMPSHIRE (403 U.S. 443: 1971), p. 162; FOURTH AMENDMENT, p. 159.

*Significance*     *Washington v. Chrisman* (455 U.S. 1: 1982) rested upon the plain view exception to the warrant requirement. *Chrisman* drew heavily upon *Harris v. United States* (390 U.S. 234: 1968) and *Coolidge v. New Hampshire* (403 U.S. 443: 1971). *Harris* involved the discovery of evidence while securing an impounded car as defined in department regulations. *Harris* held that evidence may be seized which is "in the plain view of an officer who has the right to be in a position to have that view." Controlling for *Harris* was the recognition that the officer had legally opened the door to Harris' car before finding the seized evidence. The *Harris* decision did not permit warrantless entry of a residence, however, simply because an officer notes contraband through a window. *Coolidge* sharpened *Harris* by saying that "plain view alone is never enough to justify the warrantless seizure of evidence." The exigent circumstance, however, can provide the basis for the warrantless seizure of evidence in plain view. *Coolidge* also established that plain view discoveries "must be inadvertent." Anticipated discovery cannot be included within plain view and must be handled through a warrant. *Chrisman* reiterates that legal entry by an officer must occur prior to the plain view discovery and seizure. Standing in the doorway of the students' room was a legal crossing of the "constitutionally protected threshold"; thus the seizure of the evidence noticed in plain view was permissible. A variation on the plain view theme was developed in *United States v. Jacobsen* (466 U.S. 109: 1984). Several bags of a white powder were found concealed in a tube by freight company employees as they examined a damaged package. The employees notified authorities who subjected the powder to tests without a warrant. The substance was confirmed to be cocaine. A warrant was subsequently obtained to search the location where the package was addressed. The Court held that a warrant was not necessary for the chemical test. The original discovery had been made by private persons. Thus it was not seen as official conduct subject to Fourth Amendment limitations. The subsequent inspection by law enforcement agents did not materially expand the scope of the search conducted by the freight company personnel. The law enforcement search "impinged no legitimate expectation of privacy." The Court saw the seizure of the bags as appropriate because it was apparent the bags contained contraband. Given what the agents came to know about the package, the Court found the contents to be virtually in plain view and thus seizable. Conducting the test was not seen as compromising a legitimate privacy interest because it merely disclosed whether or not the substance was cocaine.

## Automobile Searches

*United States v. Robinson*, 414 U.S. 218, 94 S.Ct. 467, 38 L.Ed. 2d 427 (1973)    Discussed whether or not a traffic violation may trigger an arrest which then provides the basis for a full search. Robinson was stopped by a police officer who had reason to believe Robinson was driving with a revoked license. Probable cause was satisfied in that the same officer had stopped Robinson only four days earlier and had found Robinson's license to have been revoked. The officer put Robinson under a full-custody arrest and conducted a thorough search. The search yielded a packet containing heroin capsules, and Robinson sought to have the evidence suppressed. The Supreme Court upheld the search in a 6–3 decision. The question faced by the Court was that though Robinson had been legally arrested, was the full search justified since it could not yield any evidence pertaining to the traffic offense? The majority argued that a custodial arrest allowed a full search and that such a situation was not bound by the limits placed on investigative searches under stop and frisk guidelines. The Court asserted that "standards traditionally governing a search incident to lawful arrest are not . . . commuted to the stricter *Terry* standards by the absence of probable fruits or further evidence of the particular crime for which the arrest is made." Further, custodial arrests subject officers to "extended exposure" to danger, more so than the "fleeting contact" of stop and frisks, thus a fuller search than a cursory weapons frisk can be justified. The majority concluded that if the arrest is lawful, authority to search is established, and the full search "is not only an exception to the warrant requirement of the Fourth Amendment, but is also a 'reasonable' search under that Amendment." The dissenters, Justices Douglas, Brennan, and Marshall, disagreed with the majority on two crucial points. First, they felt it was necessary to require establishment of probable cause relative to the seized evidence after the arrest. Without having to justify searches on a case-by-case basis, the full arrest might simply be "a pretext for searching the arrestee." Second, the dissenters rejected the argument that a search of personal effects was appropriate even if it could be justified that Robinson was required to empty his pockets. The minority could not agree that "simply because some interference with an individual's privacy and freedom of movement has lawfully taken place, further intrusions should automatically be allowed despite the absence of a warrant that the Fourth Amendment would otherwise require." *See also* CHAMBERS V. MARONEY (399 U.S. 42: 1970), p. 182; CHIMEL V. CALIFORNIA (395 U.S. 752: 1969), p. 175; FOURTH AMENDMENT, p. 159; PROBABLE CAUSE, p. 446; STOP AND FRISK, p. 455; TERRY V. OHIO (392 U.S. 1: 1968), p. 188.

*Significance*      *United States v. Robinson* (414 U.S. 218: 1973) held that a traffic violation may provide the basis for a lawful custodial arrest. The custodial arrest, in turn, permits a full warrantless search of the person and the area within the arrestee's "immediate control" incident to that lawful arrest. The primary impact of *Robinson* is found in the breadth of the warrant exception permitted. *Robinson* allowed a full search, not a search confined to discovery of weapons. The Court explicitly distinguished the situation from *Terry v. Ohio* (392 U.S. 1: 1968), and the stricter stop and frisk guidelines. The *Robinson* search was not connected to finding evidence related to the offense for which Robinson was under arrest. The search in *Robinson* also differed from such incident-to-arrest searches as in *Chimel v. California* (395 U.S. 752: 1969) in that no arrest warrant authorized Robinson's detention. The Court took *Robinson* one step further in *Gustafson v. Florida* (414 U.S. 260: 1973), decided the same day as *Robinson. Gustafson* permitted a search incident to a custodial arrest for a traffic violation even though state law and department regulations permitted the officer merely to issue a traffic citation. *Robinson* and *Gustafson* are among the more permissive decisions relative to Fourth Amendment limits upon unreasonable search conduct. *Robinson* is limited, however, to the "traffic stop" for a full custodial arrest. In *Robinson,* the officer had probable cause to believe the driver was driving on a revoked license, a serious offense in the traffic codes of all states. More generally, the traffic stop can provide sufficient cause for a variety of actions. In *New York v. Class* (89 L.Ed. 2d 81: 1986), for example, the Court ruled that the Fourth Amendment was not violated by an officer's confiscation of a gun found when he was reaching into the car to move papers obscuring the vehicle's registration number. The Court's reasons were (1) the number played an important role in the government's scheme of automobile regulation, a clearly legitimate governmental activity; (2) because the number was to be placed in plain view, the motorist had a diminished expectation of privacy; and (3) the officer had directly observed the driver commit two traffic violations. The search was limited and sufficiently unintrusive to be permissible given the lack of substantial expectation of privacy.

## Automobile Searches

*South Dakota v. Opperman,* **428 U.S. 364, 96 S.Ct. 3092, 49 L.Ed. 2d 1000 (1978)**    Involved a warrantless inventory search of an impounded automobile. Opperman's car was impounded for numerous parking violations. A police officer noted some personal property in the car, and, following established inventory practices, inventoried the contents of Opperman's car. During the inventory marijuana was discovered in the unlocked glove compartment. Opperman was subsequently prosecuted for possession of marijuana. He sought to have the evidence suppressed, but his motion was denied and he was convicted. The Supreme Court affirmed the conviction 5–4. In addition to the mobility dimension involved with automobiles, the majority stressed that there is a diminished "expectation of privacy with respect to one's automobile" as distinct from "one's home or office." The primary function of automobiles is transportation, and a car "seldom serves as one's residence or as the repository of personal effects." In the course of their "community caretaking functions," police officers often take automobiles into custody. Impounded cars are routinely secured and inventoried in order to protect the owner's property, minimize claims against police officers over lost or stolen property, and to protect police officers from potential danger. The majority found these "caretaking procedures" to be an established practice within state law. The search was not unreasonable because the inventory was "prompted by the presence in plain view of a number of valuables inside the car." Opperman never suggested that this "standard procedure, essentially like that followed throughout the country, was a pretext concealing an investigatory police motive." A dissent authored by Justice Marshall was joined by Justices Brennan, Stewart, and White. It emphasized there was "no reason to believe that the glove compartment of the impounded car contained any particular property of any substantial value." In addition the minority deferred to Opperman's locking of the car as adequate protection of his property. The police could show no further need for protection. Finally, police officers made no attempt to secure Opperman's consent. In short, the dissenters objected to the result of the holding which "elevates the conservation of property interests—indeed mere possibilities of property interests—above the privacy and security interest protected by the Fourth Amendment." *See also* CHAMBERS V. MARONEY (399 U.S. 42: 1970), p. 182; FOURTH AMENDMENT, p. 159.

*Significance*    *South Dakota v. Opperman* (428 U.S. 364: 1978) broadened permissible seizures under the plain view doctrine by approving the warrantless entry into an impounded car for purposes of conducting a standard inventory. While the Court limited the *Opperman* holding to the facts of that case, two points stand out in the opinion. First, authorities were allowed to seize criminal evidence from a car which was entered with neither a warrant nor with probable cause to believe that evidence of a crime was contained therein. The rationale was the "diminished expectation of privacy" attached to a car and the various needs served by conducting the inventory. Second, the Court suggested that such inventories ought not to be evaluated in probable cause terms. In a footnote the Court observed that the "probable cause approach is unhelpful when analysis centers upon the reasonableness of routine administrative caretaking functions." The majority maintained that *Opperman* represented "standard practice" for the police, and there existed no suggestion of any investigatory motive. Had there been such a motive, the investigation would have been a "subterfuge for criminal investigation" and would not have been permitted. Since *Opperman*, the Court has broadened the scope of permissible impoundment searches without warrant. In *Michigan v. Thomas* (458 U.S. 259: 1982), the Court upheld the warrantless search of an impounded automobile made subsequent to a routine inventory. The *Thomas* decision was reiterated in *Florida v. Myers* (466 U.S. 380: 1984). At the time of Myers' arrest, his car was searched by authorities and taken to an impound lot. Some eight hours later, a second search was conducted without a warrant. The Court upheld the second search because police officers had cause to believe evidence was still located in the car. The Court said the impoundment search was justified on the same grounds as the initial search incident to the arrest.

## Automobile Searches

*United States v. Ross,* **456 U.S. 798, 102 S.Ct. 2157, 72 L.Ed. 2d 572 (1982)**     Permitted the warrantless search of a container found in a lawfully stopped automobile. The holding in *United States v. Ross* was that as long as probable cause exists, police authority to perform a warrantless search is coextensive with a magistrate's authority to issue a warrant. Following a tip, police officers found a car in a location specified by the informant. The informant was known to the police and had provided reliable information previously. The driver of the car, Ross, matched the informant's description. The informant had said that drugs were contained in the trunk of the car. On stopping the car and opening the trunk, the police found a closed paper bag. It was opened and heroin was discovered. A zippered pouch containing cash was subsequently found as well. Ross sought to have the evidence suppressed, but he was unsuccessful and convicted. The Court of Appeals agreed with Ross, holding that the bag and pouch could not be opened in the absence of a warrant. The Supreme Court reversed the Court of Appeals in a 6–3 decision. The opinion of the Court was delivered by Justice Stevens. He traced the history of the automobile warrant exception and reiterated the impracticability of having to secure a warrant where transportation of contraband was involved. He said that relief from securing a warrant does not diminish the probable cause requirement, however. The only warrantless automobile search permissible is one "supported by probable cause." The probable cause determination must be based on objective facts that could justify the issuance of a warrant by a magistrate. The mere "subjective good faith" of a police officer is insufficient to constitute probable cause. Once the probable cause requirement has been met, the practical consequences of the automobile warrant exception would be largely nullified if the scope of the search did not include containers and packages found inside the vehicle. A warranted search of any premises extends to the entire area in which the object of the search may be found. This rule applies equally to all containers and carries over to the warrantless search of an automobile. Stevens noted that the protection of the Fourth Amendment "varies in different settings." A container that is in a person's possession at the time of arrest may be searched "even without any specific suspicion concerning its contents." The privacy interests of an individual must give way to the finding of probable cause. Stevens concluded by saying the scope of a warrantless automobile search is not defined by the nature of the container. It is defined by "the object of the search and the places in which there is probable cause to believe that it may be found." Justices White, Brennan, and Marshall dissented. Marshall said the decision repeals the Fourth Amendment warrant requirement. The value of a probable cause determination by a neutral and detached magistrate is lost by permitting police officers to make the same judgment. Marshall saw the ruling as "flatly inconsistent" with established principles concerning the scope of the automobile warrant exception. *See also CHAMBERS V. MARONEY* (399 U.S. 42: 1970), p. 182; FOURTH AMENDMENT, p. 159; *SOUTH DAKOTA V. OPPERMAN* (428 US. 364: 1978), p. 185; *UNITED STATES V. ROBINSON* (414 U.S. 218: 1973), p. 183.

*Significance*    In *United States v. Ross* (456 U.S. 798: 1982), the Court allowed the warrantless search of containers found in automobiles. The case constitutes a significant change in Court policy in this sensitive area. Prior to *Ross,* the Court had held that containers found in cars were protected unless their contents were in plain view, a rule derived from several cases having to do with the expectations of privacy attaching to luggage. In *United States v. Chadwick* (433 U.S. 1: 1977), the Court refused to permit the warrantless search of a secured footlocker taken from an automobile trunk. It said the locked container conveyed a privacy expectation that required warrant protection. In *Arkansas v. Sanders* (442 U.S. 753: 1979), the Court rejected the automobile exception as the basis for a warrantless search of anything, including a suitcase, found in the course of the examination of an automobile. Two years later, in *Robbins v. California* (453 U.S. 420: 1981), the Court held that a closed container found during a lawful automobile search was constitutionally protected to the same extent as are closed items of luggage found anywhere else. *Ross* distinguished *Chadwick* and overruled *Robbins*. The Court maintained that the *Chadwick* decision did not rest on the automobile exception because the footlocker itself "was the suspected locus of the contraband." But not all movable containers are subject to warrantless search after seizure even if they come in contact with an automobile. Thus *Ross* retained *Chadwick*. *Robbins*, on the other hand, involved cause to search a whole automobile, not just a footlocker. The *Robbins* prohibition on the search of a closed container found in the execution of the lawful search of an automobile was rejected by *Ross*. So long as probable cause exists to search an automobile, the expectation of privacy does not extend to closed containers which might be capable of concealing the object of the search. In *Illinois v. Andreas* (463 U.S. 765: 1983), the Court held that if contraband is discovered during an inspection, the container may be resealed, delivered, and reopened without a warrant after the receiver takes delivery. Finally, in *United States v. Johns* (469 U.S. 478: 1984), the Court extended *Ross* to warrantless searches occurring three days after packages were seized. Given the fact that authorities could have opened the containers at the time of the seizure under the *Ross* rule, the Court found no requirement that the containers be examined immediately.

## Stop and Frisk

***Terry v. Ohio*, 392 U.S. 1, 88 S.Ct. 1868, 20 L.Ed. 2d 889 (1968)** Examined the practice of stop and frisk and established basic guidelines for a limited warrantless search conducted on persons behaving in a suspicious manner. A police officer of 39 years' service observed two men, later joined by a third, acting "suspiciously." Specifically, the officer felt the men were "casing" a particular store. The officer approached the men, identified himself as a police officer, and requested identification. Upon receiving an unsatisfactory response to his request, the officer frisked the men. Terry was found to have a gun in his possession, and was subsequently charged and convicted for carrying a concealed weapon. The Supreme Court upheld the validity of the stop and frisk practice, with only Justice Douglas dissenting. It was admitted in *Terry* that the officer did not have "probable cause" to search. Indeed, this is why *Terry* is important in Fourth Amendment cases. The majority distinguished between a frisk and a full search. The Court concluded that the officer was entitled to conduct a cursory search for weapons. Such a search is "protective," and while it constitutes an "intrusion upon the sanctity of the person," it is briefer and more limited than a full search. The frisk was justified by the need to discover weapons which may be used to harm the officer or others. Thus, where the officer "observes unusual conduct which leads him reasonably to conclude in light of his experience that criminal activity may be afoot," where he identifies himself as a police officer, and where "nothing in the initial stages of the encounter serves to dispel his reasonable fear for his own or others' safety," he is entitled to conduct a cursory search. Justice Douglas argued that probable cause had not been satisfied with respect to the weapons charge, i.e., the officer had no basis to believe Terry was carrying a weapon; thus the search was invalid. *See also* BROWN V. TEXAS (443 U.S. 47: 1979), p. 190; FOURTH AMENDMENT, p. 159; STOP AND FRISK, p. 455.

*Significance*     *Terry v. Ohio* (392 U.S. 1: 1968) provided law enforcement authorities with the capability of executing preventive actions. Not only did *Terry* allow police to stop a person in situations deemed to be "suspicious," but *Terry* authorized a limited weapons patdown. Controlling in *Terry* was observed behavior which would justify or give cause for making the stop. Given cause to stop, the officer was entitled to conduct at least a cursory search. *Terry* does not allow a full search unless the cursory search yields a weapon which leads to an actual custodial arrest. In *Sibron v. New York* (392 U.S. 40: 1968), a case decided with *Terry*, the Court disallowed a stop and frisk which netted a package of narcotics, because the searching officer could not demonstrate cause for the stop. There was no reason to infer that Sibron was armed at the time of the stop or presented a danger to the officer. The Court felt the search of Sibron was a search for evidence, not for weapons. The Court noted this same absence of focused suspicion in the tavern frisk case, *Ybarra v. Illinois* (444 U.S. 85: 1979). The Burger Court expanded upon *Terry* in *Adams v. Williams* (407 U.S. 143: 1972) when it permitted a frisk based upon an informant tip as opposed to an officer's own observations. In *Pennsylvania v. Mimms* (434 U.S. 106: 1977) the Court held that an officer could order a lawfully detained driver out of his automobile. Once out, the *Terry* standard must still be met. The Court concluded that considerations of an officer's safety justified having a driver leave a car, and if cause exists to proceed with a frisk, a patdown is permissible. *Terry* and the cases that build upon it authorize substantial latitude for a cursory weapons search if observed or reported behavior can focus sufficient suspicion. Two recent cases further define the scope of *Terry*. In *United States v. Place* (462 U.S. 696: 1983) the Court held that suspicious luggage may be seized at an airport and subjected to a sniff test by a narcotics detection dog. In this case the permissible limits of a *Terry* search were exceeded, however, when the luggage was kept for 90 minutes, the suspect was not informed of where the luggage would be taken, and detention officers failed to specify how the luggage might be returned. *Terry* was also extended in *Michigan v. Long* (463 U.S. 1032: 1983) when the Court allowed a protective search of the passenger compartment of a stopped car. The majority ruled that "*Terry* need not be read as restricting the preventive search to the person of the detained suspect." Search of the passenger compartment of a car is permissible as long as the police "possess an articulable and objectively reasonable belief that the suspect is potentially dangerous." Contraband discovered in the course of such a protective search is admissible evidence. The Court used the reasonable suspicion standard of *Terry* to uphold searches by school officials in *New Jersey v. T.L.O.* (469 U.S. 325: 1985). The Court held that searching a student's handbag is justified if there are "reasonable grounds for suspecting" the search will yield evidence that laws or school rules are being violated. Such searches are permissible if they are related to the objectives of the search and are not excessively intrusive, given the age and sex of the student and the nature of the infraction. The Court recognized that searches are a "severe violation" of the student's privacy. It therefore urged school officials to limit their conduct "according to the dictates of reason." But the Court said society must recognize that drug use and crime are "major social problems," and that searches are justified as a means of maintaining school discipline. Although it noted that constitutional protections did apply in this case, the Court permitted the search based on the existence of reasonable suspicion. Further evolution of *Terry* occurred in *United States v. Sharpe* (470 U.S. 675: 1985), where the Court upheld short-term, i.e., 20 minute, investigative detention where reasonable suspicion exists. In *Hayes v. Florida* (470 U.S. 811: 1985), however, the Court said that police officers may not take a suspect to police headquarters for fingerprinting in the absence of probable cause, a warrant, or the person's consent. The Court left the door open for a brief detention for field administration of fingerprinting when reasonable suspicion exists. It said such detention "is not necessarily impermissible."

## Prisoners' Rights

***Block v. Rutherford*, 468 U.S. 576, 104 S.Ct. 3227, 82 L.Ed 2d 438 (1984)** Held that persons detained in a pretrial circumstance do not have the right to contact visits and can have their cells searched in their absence. *Block v. Rutherford* involved a policy of the Los Angeles County jail which denied any contact visits with relatives or friends of pretrial detainees. Also under review was the practice of jail authorities to conduct irregularly scheduled searches of individual jail cells when the occupants were not present. A number of pretrial detainees brought a class action challenging the policy and practice. The lower federal courts sustained the challenge. The Supreme Court reversed, however, in a 6–3 decision. The opinion of the Court was written by Chief Justice Burger. First, the Chief Justice described the security concerns which attended the case. The Los Angeles County jail houses some 200,000 persons annually while they await trial. Those who must be detained before trial constitute a serious security problem "given the ease with which one can obtain release on bail or personal recognizance." Holding a person before trial thus becomes "a significant factor bearing on the security measures that are imperative to proper administration of a detention facility." The Court defined the inquiry as being whether or not the challenged condition or policy constitutes punishment. Is the disability imposed for the purpose of punishment, or is it incidental to some other legitimate government purpose? Without proof of intent to punish, the issue hinges on whether there is an alternative purpose for the restriction and whether the restriction is excessive. Before applying these guidelines to *Block,* the Court expressed its belief that courts should play a very limited role in the administration of detention facilities. Prison administrators should be accorded wide-ranging deference in the adoption and execution of policies and practices that in their judgment are needed to preserve internal order and discipline and maintain institutional security. In considering the ban on contact visits, the Court focused on the question of legitimate government objective since it was conceded the prohibition was not intended as punishment. The Court found a "rational connection" between the ban and internal security at the facility. Contact visits "invite a host of security problems." They open the institution to the introduction of drugs, weapons, and other contraband. The visits also pose the danger of exposing visitors to risk from detainees awaiting trial for serious, sometimes violent offenses. In this respect, pretrial detainees are as much a security risk as convicted prisoners. The Court did not find a total ban on contact visits excessive. To attempt limited visitation for low security risk detainees would offer a difficult identification problem exacerbated by the constantly changing nature of the inmate population. Burger reiterated the Court's unwillingness "to substitute our judgment on these difficult and sensitive matters" for that of persons charged with and trained in the running of such facilities. The Court concluded that the prohibition was "an entirely reasonable, nonpunitive response to legitimate security concerns." The Court similarly deferred to the "informed discretion of prison authorities" by upholding the shakedown searches of cells conducted in the absence of detainees. Justices Brennan, Marshall, and Stevens dissented. Brennan said the Court appeared willing to sanction any prison condition for which it could imagine a "colorable rationale," no matter how oppressive or ill justified that condition is in fact. *See also* FOURTH AMENDMENT, p. 159.

*Significance*     Security reasons prompted the Court in *Block v. Rutherford* (468 U.S. 576: 1984) to hold that detention facility officials may prohibit all contact visits. For similar reasons the Court also upheld searches of detention facility cells in the absence of the detainee. While prisoners are constitutionally protected, recent decisions such as *Block* clearly indicate that the scope of their protection is more severely restricted than that of the general public. The first major case in this area was *Bell v. Wolfish* (441 U.S. 520: 1979), in which the Court upheld a variety of practices at a short-term custodial facility. Included in the permitted practices were (1) "double-bunking," or the assignment of two detainees to a cell originally designed for single occupancy; (2) limiting receipt of hardcover books to those books mailed directly from publishers or bookstores; (3) prohibiting receipt of all packages from outside the detention facility; (4) strip and body cavity searches following contact visits; and (5) unobserved cell searches. As in *Block,* the Court was highly deferential to the security and management interests of detention facility officials. The Court also noted a diminished privacy expectation for persons in such detention facilities. Two years after *Bell v. Wolfish,* the Court upheld in *Rhodes v. Chapman* (452 U.S. 337: 1981) long-term double-celling against claims that it constituted cruel and unusual punishment. In *Whitley v. Albers* (89 L.Ed. 2d 251: 1986), the Court ruled that the shooting of an inmate by a prison guard while the guard was trying to halt a prison riot was not cruel and unusual punishment either. The Court concluded that it is "obduracy and wantonness, not inadvertence or error in good faith" that characterizes conduct prohibited by the Cruel and Unusual Punishment Clause. The infliction of pain during an attempt to restore order is not prohibited by the Fourth Amendment "simply because it may appear in retrospect" that the measures taken may have been unreasonable, and hence unnecessary in the strict sense. The Court said the general requirement that a claimant establish the unnecessary and wanton infliction of pain should be applied with due regard for differences in the kind of conduct involved. In *Hudson v. Palmer* (468 U.S. 517: 1984), decided on the same day as *Block,* the court said prisoners could be subjected to random searches. If a prisoner's lawfully possessed property is destroyed during such a search, a constitutional violation occurs only if the state provides no mechanism to obtain remedy for the property lost. Chief Justice Burger said in *Hudson* that "the recognition of privacy rights for prisoners in their individual cells simply cannot be reconciled with the need for incarceration and the needs of penal institutions." These words epitomize the Burger Court's general stance in response to prisoner challenges to detention facility practices.

# 3. The Fifth Amendment

# Double Jeopardy

*Waller v. Florida*, 397 U.S. 387, 90 S.Ct. 1184, 25 L.Ed. 2d 435 (1970)   Examined the question of whether a state and a municipality are separate sovereign entities, each able to prosecute criminal offenses based on the same act. Waller was convicted of destruction of city property, an ordinance violation. The state later tried him for the theft of the property. The damage to the property had occurred while it was being illegally taken. Waller was convicted of grand larceny in the second proceeding, and he appealed on double jeopardy grounds. The Supreme Court vacated the second conviction in a unanimous decision. The Court rejected the notion that separate sovereignty between a state and a municipality is analogous to the relationship between the states and the federal government. The Court argued that political subdivisions of states have never been "considered as sovereign entities." Instead, they have been viewed as "subordinate governmental instrumentalities created by the State to assist in carrying out state governmental functions." While the Constitution permits dual prosecution of an individual for federal and state offenses stemming from the same act, Waller could not be so prosecuted by a municipal and a state government. As applied in that context, the Court said the "dual sovereignty theory is an anachronism, and the second trial constituted double jeopardy." *See also* ASHE V. SWENSON (397 U.S. 436: 1970), p. 213; BREED V. JONES (421 U.S. 519: 1975), p. 216; BULLINGTON V. MISSOURI (451 U.S. 430: 1981), p. 217; DOUBLE JEOPARDY, p. 403; FIFTH AMENDMENT, p. 201; PRICE V. GEORGIA (398 U.S. 323: 1970), p. 215.

*Significance*   *Waller v. Florida* (397 U.S. 387: 1970) said the existence of multiple instrumentalities of government below the federal level in the United States creates the potential for successive prosecutions in conflict with double jeopardy protections. The counterpart issue of successive federal-state prosecutions was first treated in *United States v. Lanza* (260 U.S. 377: 1922). *Lanza* held that successive federal-state prosecutions were permissible on dual sovereignty grounds. The two sovereignties derive "power from different sources," and are "capable of dealing with the same subject-matter within the same territory." When each level defines certain behaviors as crimes and undertakes prosecution of violators, each "is exercising its own sovereignty, not that of the other." Federal and state authorities have coordinated their activities in recent years, and, as a general practice, the federal government does not commence prosecutions in cases where state prosecutions have been initiated. For the same reasons of dual sovereignty, the double jeopardy prohibition does not preclude simultaneous prosecutions in two or more states if the criminal act occurred in more than one state. A recent example of this is *Heath v. Alabama* (88 L.Ed. 2d 387: 1985). Heath had contracted for the murder of his wife. She was kidnapped from his Alabama home, killed, and her body abandoned in Georgia. After pleading guilty to a murder charge in Georgia, Heath sought to prohibit his indictment on a similar charge in Alabama on double jeopardy grounds. The Court permitted successive prosecutions by the two states for the same criminal conduct. The Court said each state possesses its own "inherent sovereignty" preserved by the Tenth Amendment. Given their distinct sources of power to prosecute, the states are "no less sovereign with respect to each other than they are with respect to the Federal Government." The Court came to the far-reaching conclusion that to deny a state power to enforce its criminal laws because another state "won the race to the courthouse" would be "a shocking and untoward deprivation" of states' rights and obligations to maintain peace and order within their boundaries. Because sovereignty flows from the source of authority, the dual sovereignty concept cannot apply in the *Waller* case, however, because local units of government are creations of state power. Conclusion of a criminal proceeding in a municipal jurisdiction or a state court constitutionally precludes a subsequent prosecution for the same criminal act in the other.

## Double Jeopardy

*Price v. Georgia*, **398 U.S. 323, 90 S.Ct. 1757, 26 L.Ed. 2d 300 (1970)**    Involved the concept of "implicit acquittal" by which it can be said that if a jury chooses to convict an individual on a lesser included charge, the jury acquitted the individual on the greater charge. Price was convicted of manslaughter, although the state had charged him with murder. Price appealed his conviction on jury instruction grounds and had his conviction set aside by a Georgia appellate court. Price was then retried with the indictment again charging him with murder. The jury again convicted Price of manslaughter, and Price appealed on double jeopardy grounds claiming impermissible jeopardy on the murder charge in the second trial. The Supreme Court agreed with Price in a unanimous decision. Justice Blackmun did not participate. Chief Justice Burger wrote for the majority that "the first verdict, limited as it was to the lesser included offense, required that the retrial be limited to that lesser offense." The Chief Justice emphasized that the double jeopardy protection "flows inescapably" from a concern about "risk of conviction," and Price was "twice put in jeopardy." Price's jeopardy on the murder charge "ended when the first jury 'was given a full opportunity to return a verdict' on that charge and instead reached a verdict on a lesser charge." Burger concluded the opinion by suggesting that there was no effective difference between a direct or explicit acquittal and one "implied by a conviction on a lesser included offense when the jury was given a full opportunity to return a verdict on the greater charge." See also ASHE V. SWENSON (397 U.S. 436: 1970), p. 213; BREED V. JONES (421 U.S. 519: 1975), p. 216; BULLINGTON V. MISSOURI (451 U.S. 430: 1981), p. 217; DOUBLE JEOPARDY, p. 403; FIFTH AMENDMENT, p. 201; WALLER V. FLORIDA (397 U.S. 387: 1970), p. 212.

*Significance*     *Price v. Georgia* (398 U.S. 323: 1970) raises and settles the question of implicit acquittal, but it also addresses the more general question of the extent to which double jeopardy protection applies to a case where a defendant successfully appeals a conviction. Reprosecution is typically permitted. The Court advanced a waiver rationale in *Green v. United States* (355 U.S. 184: 1957), saying that an appealing defendant is waiving double jeopardy protection by requesting that the conviction be reversed. Although the waiver argument is not wholly persuasive, and while some cases subsequent to *Green* have seemed to temper the waiver approach, defendants remain vulnerable to the reinstitution of charges following a successful appeal. The exception to the retrial rule applies to those cases where the successful appeal has determined that the conviction was based on legally deficient evidence. The "implicit acquittal" principle of *Price* applies at this point. It limits the charge on reprosecution to no greater than the equivalent of the original conviction. Thus, if a jury opted to convict to a lesser included level at the initial trial, the retrial is limited to a charge no more serious than that lesser included offense. *Price* sets the limitation on the scope of reprosecution following a successful appeal. On a related matter, the Court ruled in *Ohio v. Johnson* (467 U.S. 493: 1984) that the double jeopardy clause did not preclude prosecution for offenses not included in a guilty plea to other charges stemming from the same indictment. Johnson was indicted for four offenses. Over the prosecution's objection, he pled guilty to two of the charges at his arraignment. The trial judge dismissed the two remaining charges on the ground that further prosecution would constitute double jeopardy. The Supreme Court reversed the trial judge, ruling that dismissal of the remaining and more serious charges did more than prevent cumulative punishment—it precluded a verdict on the charges. Johnson had not been "exposed to conviction" on the charges to which he did not plead, and the state is entitled to have an opportunity to marshal its evidence on these charges. Acceptance of the pleas to lesser included offenses does not have implications of implied acquittal. The overreaching of government is not involved, so double jeopardy does not apply. But a new trial is not always required. In *Morris v. Mathews* (89 L.Ed. 2d 187: 1986), the Court held that the modification of a double jeopardy-barred conviction to a lesser-included offense that was not barred by double jeopardy was an adequate remedy. Mathews and another person robbed a bank and fled to a farmhouse. Shots were fired inside the farmhouse and Mathews then surrendered. His companion was found dead. The death was ruled a suicide by the coroner and Mathews was charged only with robbery. He pled guilty to that charge. Subsequently, Mathews admitted killing his companion, and the state indicted him for aggravated murder in connection with the robbery. He was convicted of the aggravated murder charge. An appeals court barred the conviction for aggravated murder on double jeopardy grounds and modified the conviction to that of the lesser offense of murder. The Court said that under such circumstances the burden shifts to the defendant to demonstrate a reasonable probability that he would not have been convicted on the nonbarred offense "absent the presence of the jeopardy-barred offense."

## Self-Incrimination

***Miranda v. Arizona*, 384 U.S. 436, 86 S.Ct. 1602, 16 L.Ed. 2d 694 (1966)** Examined custodial interrogation practices. The *Miranda* decision was based on the relationship between the Fifth Amendment's privilege against self-incrimination and the Sixth Amendment's right to counsel in the pretrial period. The groundwork for *Miranda* began two years earlier in *Escobedo v. Illinois* (378 U.S. 478: 1964). In a controversial 5–4 decision, the Court overturned the conviction of Escobedo, holding that when a police investigation begins to focus on a particular individual, and when interrogation turns from mere information gathering to eliciting a confession, the American legal system requires that the individual must be allowed to consult with legal counsel. *Miranda* and three companion cases allowed the Warren Court to develop this theme further and broaden its application. The Court was particularly concerned with the interrogation environment, believing it to be a closed process and inherently coercive. Chief Justice Warren said, "Even without employing brutality . . . the very fact of custodial interrogation exacts a heavy toll on individual liberty and trades on the weaknesses of individuals." He added, "It is obvious that such an interrogation environment is created for no other purpose than to subjugate the individual to the will of the examiner. This atmosphere carries its own badge of intimidation." The majority specified four warnings which must be administered at the time of arrest, prior to beginning interrogation. The "Miranda Rules" require that an arrested person (1) be told of his or her right to remain silent; (2) be told that anything he or she says can be used against the accused in court; (3) be told that he or she has a right to consult with an attorney prior to questioning and that failure to request counsel does not constitute waiver of the right; and (4) be told that counsel will be provided to the accused in the event that he or she cannot afford counsel. *Miranda v. Arizona* (384 U.S. 436: 1966) held that statements made by the accused without these warnings are inadmissible in a trial. *See also BREWER V. WILLIAMS* (430 U.S. 387: 1977), p. 223; *ESTELLE V. SMITH* (451 U.S. 454: 1981), p. 227; *HARRIS V. NEW YORK* (401 U.S. 222: 1971), p. 220; *MICHIGAN V. TUCKER* (417 U.S. 433: 1974), p. 222; *NORTH CAROLINA V. BUTLER* (441 U.S. 369: 1979), p. 225; SELF-INCRIMINATION, p. 448.

*Significance*     *Miranda v. Arizona* (384 U.S. 436: 1966) instituted extensive changes in constitutional policy involving rights of the accused. No single decision of the Warren Court has had more impact, except perhaps *Mapp v. Ohio* (367 U.S. 643: 1961). The Warren Court clearly assigned high priority to confronting inappropriate police practices. It recognized the utility of defense counsel as a means of discouraging misconduct. Basically it tried to give meaning to constitutional protections and to prevent them from becoming empty formalisms. Protection against self-incrimination, for example, could be achieved by extending the right to counsel to critical pretrial stages; hence the linkage of the two provisions in *Miranda*. The decision intensified criticism of the Warren Court's approach to defining rights of the accused. The Court's detractors felt that *Miranda* made confessions virtually impossible to secure, thus handcuffing law enforcement authorities. Many felt the Court had preempted legislative prerogatives in setting law enforcement standards. The negative feeling toward *Miranda* was manifested in the Omnibus Crime Control Act of 1968. Provisions of this legislation softened some of the *Miranda* requirements, at least at the federal level. Federal judges, for example, were given greater latitude in determining the voluntariness of incriminating statements. It was left to the Burger Court to determine the status of *Miranda* for state trials. Several Burger Court decisions have narrowed the scope of its provisions. In *Harris v. New York* (401 U.S. 222: 1971), for example, the Court held that a statement judged inadmissible because of *Miranda* defects could be used to impeach a defendant should he or she take the witness stand. The Burger Court rejected opportunities to overrule *Miranda*, however, and embarked on a case-by-case examination of *Miranda* standards. In *Miller v. Fenton* (88 L.Ed. 2d 405: 1985), for example, it held that the voluntariness of a confession is not an issue entitled to presumption. It is rather a question meriting independent consideration in a federal court review. Thus the provisions of the United States Code that presume state court findings to be correct in *habeas corpus* proceedings do not restrict fresh federal inquiry as they do in search issues. [See *Stone v. Powell* (428 U.S. 465: 1976), p. 173.]

## Self-Incrimination

***Harris v. New York*, 401 U.S. 222, 91 S.Ct. 643, 28 L.Ed. 2d 1 (1971)** Considered whether statements made by a defendant in violation of *Miranda* could be used to impeach that defendant's own testimony at his or her trial. *Miranda* established that criminal defendants must be informed of their right against self-incrimination and their right to assistance of counsel. While Harris was testifying at his own trial, he was asked during cross-examination whether he had made any statements immediately following his arrest. When he claimed he could not recall making any statements, the statements he in fact made were introduced into evidence for the purpose of impeaching Harris' credibility. The jury instruction attempted to differentiate between use of statements for impeachment purposes and their use as evidence of guilt. The jury was instructed it could not do the latter. Harris was subsequently convicted. The Supreme Court rejected his appeal in a 5–4 decision. The majority said that *Miranda* is not an absolute prohibition against the use of statements taken without proper warnings. *Miranda* bars the prosecution from "making its case with statements" taken in violation of *Miranda*. But "it does not follow from *Miranda* that evidence inadmissible against an accused in the prosecution's case in chief is barred for all purposes." Use of such evidence, however, must satisfy conditions of trustworthiness. Crucial to the outcome in *Harris* is the use of statements made in an adversary process: specifically, impeachment of a witness through cross-examination. The "impeachment process here undoubtedly provided valuable aid to the jury in assessing petitioner's credibility." The majority felt that information was of more value than guarding against the "speculative possibility" that police misconduct would be encouraged.

The majority emphasized the need to maintain the integrity of the trial itself. A defendant can testify in his own defense but does not have "the right to commit perjury." Once the defendant takes the witness stand, the prosecution can "utilize the traditional truth-testing devices of the adversary process." Chief Justice Burger concluded the opinion by saying, "The shield provided by *Miranda* cannot be perverted into a license to use perjury by way of a defense, free from the risk of confrontation with prior inconsistent utterances." The dissenters— Justices Douglas, Black, Brennan, and Marshall—argued that tainted statements should not be used under any circumstance. They felt the decision would "seriously undermine" the maintenance of constitutional protections against police misconduct. *See also* BREWER V. WILLIAMS (430 U.S. 387: 1977), p. 223; FIFTH AMENDMENT, p. 201; MICHIGAN V. TUCKER (417 U.S. 433: 1974), p. 222; MIRANDA V. ARIZONA (384 U.S. 436: 1966), p. 219; NORTH CAROLINA V. BUTLER (441 U.S. 369: 1979), p. 225; SELF-INCRIMINATION, p. 448; STONE V. POWELL (428 U.S. 465: 1976), p. 173.

*Significance*     *Harris v. New York* (401 U.S. 222: 1971) seriously qualified *Miranda*. The Court allowed *Miranda*-defective statements and confessions to be utilized to impeach a defendant, as opposed to being used in making the case in chief. *Harris* reflects the Burger Court's reluctance to fully embrace the *Miranda* holding, as well as its general unwillingness to disturb the dynamics of the adversary process. The basic thrust of *Harris* is that a jury ought to be given every opportunity to assess a defendant and the defense being advanced. The underlying theme of *Harris* was reiterated in *Oregon v. Hass* (420 U.S. 714: 1975) by a 6–2 margin. The *Harris-Hass* rule does not apply, however, where statements are obtained involuntarily. In *Mincey v. Arizona* (437 U.S. 385: 1978), the Court ruled that interrogation of a defendant hospitalized in critical condition produced involuntary and untrustworthy responses. They could not be used even for impeachment purposes. The Court has also held that postwarning silence cannot be used to impeach a defendant. In *Doyle v. Ohio* (426 U.S. 610: 1976), two defendants offered exculpatory explanations at their trial, explanations not previously shared with police officers or prosecutors. They were cross-examined as to why they had withheld their stories until the trial. A six-justice majority concluded that "silence in the wake of these [*Miranda*] warnings may be nothing more than the arrestee's exercise of these *Miranda* rights." On the other hand, silence occurring previous to receiving *Miranda* warnings may be used for impeachment purposes on the grounds that the silence was not "induced by the assurances contained in the *Miranda* warnings." In *Wainwright v. Greenfield* (88 L.Ed. 2d 623: 1986), the Court ruled that a suspect's silence after receiving the *Miranda* warnings could not be used as evidence to counter his insanity defense. A unanimous Court said the source of unfairness is the assurance contained in the *Miranda* warnings that silence will carry no penalty. It is fundamentally unfair to promise a person that silence will not be used against him or her and then breach that promise by using silence to overcome a defendant's plea of insanity. In *Oregon v. Elstad* (470 U.S. 298: 1985) the Court opined that a voluntary admission coming prior to *Miranda* warnings does not necessarily require suppression of a confession coming later. At the time of his arrest, Elstad incriminated himself before receiving any warnings. He made statements voluntarily, in the presence of his mother, and in an environment that could be characterized as noncoercive. He was subsequently taken to the sheriff's office and advised of his rights. Elstad waived his rights and confessed again. While the initial statements were unquestionably inadmissible, Elstad later argued that his sheriff's office confession was tainted by the statements made prior to receiving any warnings. The Supreme Court disagreed, saying that as long as the initial statements were voluntary, the later confession need not be suppressed. A defendant who responds to "unwarned yet uncoercive questioning is not disabled from waiving his warnings." In circumstances such as these, "thorough administration of *Miranda* warnings serves to cure the condition that rendered the unwarned statement inadmissible."

## Self-Incrimination

***Brewer v. Williams*, 430 U.S. 387, 97 S.Ct. 1232, 51 L. Ed. 2d 424 (1977)**      Involved incriminating statements made by a defendant in the absence of his attorney. Williams was arrested, arraigned, and jailed in Davenport, Iowa, for abducting and murdering a young child in the city of Des Moines. Williams consulted with attorneys in both cities and was advised to make no statements to the police. As Williams was being transported from Davenport to Des Moines, he indicated unwillingness to be interrogated until his attorney was present, but said he would make a full statement at that time. Nonetheless, one of the officers, aware that Williams was a former mental patient and deeply religious, sought to elicit statements from Williams relative to the location of the child's body. The officer suggested to Williams that the child's parents were entitled to a "Christian burial" for their child. Williams eventually made a number of incriminating statements and directed the police to the location of the child's body. Williams was subsequently tried and convicted. Evidence relating to statements made during his transportation to Des Moines were admitted at his trial over his objections. The Supreme Court held 5–4 that the evidence was inadmissible and the conviction void. The decision hinged on whether Williams had knowingly and intelligently waived his right to counsel. There was no dispute that the police officer had deliberately attempted to elicit information from Williams and that the "Christian burial speech" was "tantamount to interrogation." The majority concluded that the right to counsel had not been waived. It said that waiver required "not merely comprehension but relinquishment." That the defendant had relied heavily on advice of counsel throughout, that he had consulted with attorneys at both ends of his trip, and that he had specifically mentioned making a statement *after* completing the trip and consulting with his attorney, all were evidence of his unwillingness to waive his right to counsel. The officer elicited incriminating statements "despite Williams' express and implicit assertions of his right to counsel." Regardless of the "senseless and brutal" character of the offense, what had occurred was "so clear a violation" of Williams' constitutional protection that it "cannot be condoned." The dissenters were outraged. Chief Justice Burger called the result "intolerable." The dissenters held that Williams had not been compelled or coerced. Further, they noted that Williams' guilt was beyond doubt, and that to apply "the draconian judicial doctrine" called the exclusionary rule to cases such as *Williams* was highly inappropriate. *See also* EXCLUSIONARY RULE, p. 409; FIFTH AMENDMENT, p. 201; *HARRIS V. NEW YORK* (401 U.S. 222: 1971), p. 220; *MICHIGAN V. TUCKER* (417 U.S. 433: 1974), p. 222; *MIRANDA V. ARIZONA* (384 U.S. 436: 1966), p. 219; *NORTH CAROLINA V. BUTLER* (441 U.S. 369: 1979), p. 225; SELF-INCRIMINATION, p. 448.

*Significance*    *Brewer v. Williams* (430 U.S. 387: 1977) highlights the relationship between assistance of counsel and the protection against self-incrimination. The Court established in *Miranda* that preservation of the privilege against self-incrimination is best accomplished by providing an accused with access to defense counsel. *Brewer* conveys that the Court is reluctant to allow waiver of counsel in interrogation situations. *Brewer* also raised questions about what constitutes interrogation. The Court found the "Christian burial speech" to be intentionally designed to elicit incriminating statements. But *Brewer* did not fully define what constitutes an interrogation. The Court held that *Miranda* safeguards apply when interactions occur that the police know may reasonably be expected to elicit an incriminating response. Thus warnings must be given whenever an officer, through any action verbal or otherwise, is likely to prompt an incriminating response. The Court has held firm on the counsel waiver issue. It will not accept a voluntary confession from a defendant after he or she has requested defense counsel and the counsel is not present for the confession. In *Oregon v. Bradshaw* (462 U.S. 1039: 1983) the Court did rule, however, that a prisoner's question, "Well, what is going to happen to me now?" constituted initiation of further conversation which could yield admissible statements against him. The Court has frequently reiterated that once counsel is requested by an arrestee, interrogation cannot continue or be resumed in the absence of that counsel. The decisive issue is police-initiated action designed to elicit incriminating statements. The case of *Maine v. Moulton* (88 L.Ed. 2d 481: 1985) illustrates this principle. Moulton, represented by retained counsel, was indicted with a codefendant for several counts of theft. The codefendant met separately with police, gave a full confession, and agreed to testify against Moulton. The police subsequently arranged to "wire" the codefendant and have him meet with Moulton ostensibly to plan defense strategy. Moulton made incriminating statements at the meeting which were later admitted at his trial. The Court reversed Moulton's conviction because he was denied assistance of counsel. Counsel was said to be essential to the safeguarding of other procedural rights, especially the right against self-incrimination. When the police had the codefendant wear the transmitter to the meeting with Moulton, they knew Moulton would make statements he had a right not to make to their agent before consulting with counsel. By not telling Moulton that the codefendant was an agent of the police, they denied him his right to assistance of counsel. In *Edwards v. Arizona* (451 U.S. 477: 1981), the Court refused to allow admission of a confession obtained the day following a defendant's request for counsel. Even the rereading of the *Miranda* warnings was insufficient to overcome the failure to have counsel present. Once the right to assistance of counsel is invoked, no subsequent conversation may occur except on the defendant's initiative. The reasoning in *Edwards* was also applied in *Michigan v. Jackson* (89 L.Ed. 2d 631: 1986). Following his arraignment on a murder charge, Jackson requested that counsel be appointed. Before he could meet with his lawyer, police officers administered *Miranda* warnings to Jackson and interrogated him. The interrogation yielded a confession. The Court said that when the officers initiated the interview after the defendant requested counsel "at an arraignment or similar proceeding," any subsequent waiver of the right to counsel for that police-initiated interrogation is invalid. In *Shea v. Louisiana* (470 U.S. 51: 1985), the Court held that the *Edwards* rule applied to cases pending on direct appeal at the time *Edwards* was decided.

## Self-Incrimination

*North Carolina v. Butler,* 441 U.S. 369, 99 S.Ct. 1755, 60 L.Ed. 2d
286 (1979)    Considered whether the waiver of a constitutional
right need be explicit. Butler was arrested and informed of his *Miranda*
rights. He was given an "Advice of Rights" form which he read and said
he understood. He refused, however, to sign the waiver provision at the
bottom of the form, although he indicated he was "willing to talk."
Butler subsequently tried to have statements made during the ensuing
conversation suppressed. The case revolved around a determination of
whether Butler had actually waived his rights. The Supreme Court
decided that Butler's statements could be admitted. The majority in an
opinion written by Justice Stewart, joined by Chief Justice Burger and
Justices White, Blackmun, and Rehnquist, held that while explicit
waiver is usually strong proof of the validity of a waiver, it is not
"inevitably either necessary or sufficient to establish waiver." The Court
said further, "The question is not one of form, but rather whether the
defendant in fact knowingly and voluntarily waived the rights delineated in *Miranda.*" The burden of demonstrating the adequacy of a
waiver rests with the prosecution, and the prosecution's "burden is
great." However, "in at least some cases waiver can be clearly inferred
from the actions and words of the person interrogated." Waivers must
be evaluated in terms of the facts and circumstances of each case. The
Court's judgment was that Butler made a knowing and voluntary
waiver even though it was not explicit. The majority clearly rejected the
establishment of an "inflexible *per se* rule" requiring explicit waiver. The
dissenters—Justices Brennan, Marshall, and Stevens—argued that an
affirmative or explicit waiver is required to satisfy *Miranda.* Justice
Powell did not participate in the case. The dissenting justices claimed
that *Miranda* recognized that custodial interrogation is "inherently
coercive," and that ambiguity must be "interpreted against the inter-
rogator." They would have required a "simple prophylactic rule requiring the police to obtain express waiver." *See also* BREWER V. WILLIAMS
(430 U.S. 387: 1977), p. 223; FIFTH AMENDMENT, p. 201; HARRIS V. NEW
YORK (410 U.S. 222: 1971), p. 220; MICHIGAN V. TUCKER (417 U.S. 433:
1974), p. 222; MIRANDA V. ARIZONA (384 U.S. 436: 1966), p. 219; SELF-
INCRIMINATION, p. 448.

*Significance*    *North Carolina v. Butler* (441 U.S. 369: 1979) specifies
what must be done by a defendant to waive the associated rights of
assistance of counsel and protection against self-incrimination. The
*Miranda* protections may be waived, but the waiver must be voluntary,
knowing, and intelligent. It may not be the product of coercion, trick,

threat, persuasion, or inducement. While the waiver need not be written or explicit, it cannot be presumed from silence under any circumstances. The burden rests with the prosecution to demonstrate that a waiver was freely, knowingly, and intelligently made. Determinations of the adequacy of a waiver are to be based on the "totality of the circumstances" of a particular case and may include such matters as the background and overall conduct of the defendant. *Butler* provides some latitude by not requiring a firm rule relative to explicit waiver. At the same time it clarifies and maintains the general protections afforded by *Miranda*. The latter was intended to draw a clear and bright line obviating the need for a case-by-case determination of voluntariness. *Butler* brings the Court full circle. The dissent recognizes that *Butler* implicitly, if not explicitly, overruled part of *Miranda*'s clear holding. The governing role of a valid waiver is reflected in *Moran v. Burbine* (89 L.Ed. 2d 410: 1986). Burbine was arrested for breaking and entering. The police subsequently came to believe that he was involved in a murder in another community. Officers from the second community were notified, and they came to question Burbine about the murder. In the meantime, and unknown to Burbine, his sister was arranging for counsel on the breaking and entering charge. Neither Burbine's sister nor the public defender she obtained knew anything about the murder charge. Counsel contacted the police indicating that she was ready to represent Burbine if the police wished to question him. She was told he would not be questioned further until the next day. She was not told that police from the second community were present and ready to begin their questioning of Burbine. He was given *Miranda* warnings before each of three interview sessions. He signed waivers prior to each and proceeded to sign admissions to the murder. At no time was Burbine aware of his sister's arrangement of counsel or the attorney's telephone call. Yet in a 6–3 decision, the Court allowed use of the confessions. It said the police followed "with precision" the *Miranda* procedure for obtaining the waivers. The failure to inform Burbine of the attorney's call did not deprive him of information essential to his ability to make a knowing and voluntary waiver. Events taking place outside his presence and unknown to him "can have no bearing on the capacity to comprehend and knowingly relinquish a constitutional right." As long as it could be shown that his waiver was uncoerced and that he knew he did not have to speak and could request counsel, the waiver was valid. The Court said *Miranda* would not be extended to require reversal of convictions if police are "less than forthright" in dealing with an attorney or if they fail to inform the suspect of the attorney's unilateral efforts to contact him or her. The purpose of *Miranda* is to "dissipate the compulsion inherent in custodial interrogation" and thus protect the *suspect's* Fifth Amendment rights. A rule that focuses on how police treat an *attorney*—conduct which has no relevance to the matter of compulsion of the defendant—would "ignore both *Miranda*'s mission and its only source of legitimacy."

## Inevitable Discovery

*Nix v. Williams,* **467 U.S. 431, 104 S.Ct. 2501, 81 L.Ed. 2d 377 (1984)** Decided that improperly obtained evidence may become admissible if inevitably it would have been discovered by lawful means. *Nix v. Williams* involved use at retrial of evidence derived from a conversation with the defendant conducted by police in the absence of counsel. Based on this improper interrogation, Williams' initial conviction was reversed in *Brewer v. Williams* (430 U.S. 387: 1977, p. 223). The critical disclosure during the improper conversation was the location of a murder victim's body. At the retrial, the state was permitted to use evidence pertaining to the condition of the body, articles of clothing worn by the victim, and results of various tests made on the victim's body. On *habeas corpus* review, a United States District Court upheld use of the evidence, saying the victim's body would inevitably have been found in virtually the same condition as it was when Williams led authorities to it. The Court of Appeals reversed the District Court. The Supreme Court reversed again in a 7–2 decision, holding the evidence to be admissible. The opinion of the Court was delivered by Chief Justice Burger. He said the issue before the Court was whether to adopt the "so-called ultimate or inevitable discovery exception to the Exclusionary Rule." First Burger reviewed the rationale for extending the rule to evidence that is the fruit of unlawful police conduct. The "admittedly drastic and socially costly course" of implementing the exclusionary rule is necessary to deter police from violations of constitutional and statutory protections. Accordingly, the prosecution is not to be put in a better position than it would have been without such improper conduct as may be excepted from the exclusionary rule. At the same time, the exclusionary rule has never been seen as an absolute bar to improperly obtained evidence. Burger noted the independent source exception. While finding it not directly applicable in *Nix,* he saw its underlying rationale as wholly consistent with an inevitable discovery exception. When evidence is challenged as being the product of illegal governmental activity, judicial inquiry is not confined to the issue of misconduct alone. If the prosecution can show by preponderance of evidence that information ultimately or inevitably would have been discovered by lawful means, then "the deterrence rationale has so little basis that the evidence should be admissible." Burger pointed out that three lower courts had concluded the police search was sufficiently systematic, had adequate personnel, and was sufficiently proximate to the actual location of the victim's body to be satisfied of ultimate discovery without Williams' help. Finally, the Court held that the prosecution need not prove the absence of bad faith in originally obtaining the evidence. To do so would place the courts in a position of "withholding from juries relevant and undoubted truth" that would have been available without the misconduct. Suppression under such circumstances would do nothing whatever to promote the integrity of the trial process and would inflict a wholly unacceptable burden on the administration of criminal justice. Justices Brennan and Marshall dissented. Brennan argued that "zealous efforts to emasculate the exclusionary rule" lose sight of the distinction between inevitable discovery and the independent source exception. Independence of source requires a showing that evidence was gained by lawful means, while inevitably discovered evidence has not yet achieved independent source status. The dissenters saw the inevitable discovery exception as compatible with the Constitution, but they preferred a heightened burden of proof, including "clear and convincing evidence," before allowing evidence to be admissible under this exception. *See also* EXCLUSIONARY RULE, p. 409.

*Significance* The Court established in *Nix v. Williams* (467 U.S. 431: 1984) that unlawfully obtained evidence may be used if it ultimately or inevitably would have been discovered legally. *Nix* is one of several recent Burger Court decisions which ease the admission of evidence obtained through conversations with defendants. Most of the decisions have taken the form of exceptions to *Miranda v. Arizona* (384 U.S. 486: 1966). In *Minnesota v. Murphy* (465 U.S. 420: 1984), for example, the Court allowed the use of statements made by a probationer to his probation officer despite the probationer having received no warning about the statements' admissibility in a subsequent trial. The Court said that Murphy was not really in custody and thus did not require the *Miranda* warnings. Further, the obligation to report to his probation officer did not convert otherwise voluntary statements into compelled ones. The Court fashioned a public safety exception to *Miranda* in *New York v. Quarles* (467: U.S. 649: 1984). The Court said that in some situations concern for public safety must take precedence over the need to administer *Miranda*. In *Quarles,* arresting police officers first inquired about the location of a weapon Quarles was known to be carrying. After the weapon was found, the officers administered the *Miranda* warnings. The Court said that *Miranda* did not need to be applied in all its rigor when police conduct is reasonably prompted by such a concern for public safety. Finally, in *Berkomer v. McCarty* (468

U.S. 420: 1984), the Court held that while *Miranda* is required for custodial interrogation of a person accused of a misdemeanor traffic offense, the warnings are not required for the roadside questioning of a person. In the latter situation, the motorist is not in custody, the questioning is of short duration, and it is public enough to reduce the potential for police misconduct.

## Blood Samples

*Schmerber v. California,* **384 U.S. 757, 86 S.Ct. 1826, 16 L.Ed. 2d 908 (1966)** Explored whether the privilege against self-incrimination extends to defendant-derived evidence of a noncommunicated nature. The privilege clearly covers communicated testimony. *Schmerber* involved a driving-while-intoxicated conviction in which critical evidence against the defendant came in the form of blood test results. The blood sample upon which the tests were performed was taken over Schmerber's objection. Schmerber challenged the conviction on search, self-incrimination, assistance of counsel, and general due process grounds. A five-justice majority rejected all of his contentions. The majority held that taking the blood sample "constituted compulsion for the purposes of the privilege." The critical question in *Schmerber* was whether or not the blood sample actually constituted making Schmerber "a witness against himself." The Court concluded that the scope of the self-incrimination protection did not extend far enough to reach Schmerber. The privilege applied only to compelling evidence against the accused "from his own mouth." The evidence must be testimonial, i.e., the words or communications of the accused. The majority likened the blood sample to fingerprints and other means of identification. It said that making the suspect provide "real or physical evidence does not violate it" (the privilege against self-incrimination). The Court opined that in Schmerber's case, "not even a shadow of testimonial compulsion upon or enforced communication by the accused was involved either in extraction or in chemical analysis." Schmerber's "testimonial capacities were in no way implicated." In the majority's view, Schmerber, "except as a donor, was irrelevant to the results of the test." Dissents were written by Chief Justice Warren and Justices Douglas, Fortas, and Black. The dissents ranged across the issues raised by Schmerber, but Justice Black's argument was representative of the minority's concerns about self-incrimination. He said, "To reach the conclusion that compelling a person to give his blood to help the State convict him is not equivalent to compelling him to be a witness against himself strikes me as quite an extraordinary feat." The dissenters rejected the majority's distinction

between verbal testimony and physical evidence. *See also* FIFTH AMEND-
MENT, p. 201: *MANSON V. BRAITHWAITE* (432 U.S. 98: 1977), p. 232; *NEIL V.
BIGGERS* (409 U.S. 188: 1972), p. 230.

*Significance*    *Schmerber v. California* (384 U.S. 757: 1966) is the defini-
tive ruling on blood samples and self-incrimination. *Schmerber* held
simply that blood samples, because they are not testimonial in character, are not covered by the privilege against self-incrimination. As long
as the sample is not taken in a manner which "shocks the conscience,"
analysis conducted on the sample is admissible evidence. The Court has
also permitted states to admit into evidence a person's refusal to submit
to a blood-alcohol test. In *South Dakota v. Neville* (459 U.S. 553: 1983),
the Court held that since the offer of taking the test is "clearly legitimate, the action becomes no less legitimate when the State offers a
second option of refusing the test, with attendant penalties for making
that choice." In *California v. Trombetta* (467 U.S. 479: 1984), the Court
ruled that authorities are not required to preserve breath samples used
to test for intoxication. Due process considerations do not require the
samples as a necessary prerequisite to the introduction of breath-
analysis test results at trial. The Court did not interpret *Trombetta* as an
example of evidence being destroyed in a calculated effort to subvert
due process. Failure to preserve the breath samples was a good faith
action based on normal and established practice. More generally, the
Court said that the need to preserve evidence is limited to that which is
expected to play a significant role in the suspect's defense. In *Trombetta*,
the defendants had "alternative means of demonstrating their innocence" beyond the samples themselves. Use of test results based on
urine, skin, and other samples obtained from a suspect's body are also
covered under the *Schmerber* decision. This includes bullets. In *Winston
v. Lee* (470 U.S. 753: 1985), a suspect was compelled to have a bullet
removed from his body. The Court found this to be an unreasonable
search because it could not be justified against the risk created by
having to administer a general anesthetic to perform the surgery.
Extending *Schmerber,* the Court has held that samples of a person's
handwriting or voice may be used for identification purposes. In *Gilbert
v. California* (388 U.S. 263: 1967), the Court said that while one's voice
and handwriting are a means of communication, a sample of handwriting or a voice exemplar, independent of the content of what is written
or said, is an "identifying physical characteristic" which is outside the
protection of the privilege against self-incrimination. Warren Court
decisions such as *Schmerber* and *Gilbert* clearly distinguish protected
testimonial incrimination from unprotected nontestimonial evidence.
The Burger Court maintained that distinction. The only constraints on
nontestimonial evidence stemmed from the Fourth Amendment and
its guidelines governing seizure of evidence.

# 4. The Sixth Amendment

## Speedy Trial

***Barker v. Wingo,*** **407 U.S. 514, 92 S.Ct. 2182, 33 L.Ed. 2d 101 (1972)** Established criteria by which claims of denial of speedy trial may be evaluated. *Klopfer v. North Carolina* (386 U.S. 213: 1967) had already decided that the speedy trial provisions of the Sixth Amendment applied to the states. Defendant Barker was charged with murder and had a trial date set. Between the original trial date of October 21, 1958, and October 23, 1963, Barker's trial was continued 17 times. Barker did not object to the first 11 continuances because he was on pretrial release throughout most of the period. When eventually tried, Barker was convicted and sentenced to life. The Supreme Court unanimously upheld Barker's conviction. Before fashioning a speedy trial test in the case, Justice Powell considered the unique character of the speedy trial protection. He called it "generically different" from other constitutional protections because there is a "societal interest in providing a speedy trial which exists separate from, and at times in opposition to, the interests of the accused." The speedy trial concept is also more "amorphous" and "vague" than other rights of the accused. Writing for the Court, Justice Powell rejected specific timetables and the "on demand" approach as inflexible. Instead he devised a "balancing test" for evaluating speedy trial claims. The test contained four elements and "compels courts to approach speedy trial cases on an *ad hoc* basis." The four factors identified are (1) length of delay; (2) reasons offered by the government (prosecution) to justify the delay; (3) the defendant's assertion of his or her right to a speedy trial; and (4) prejudice to the defendant in terms of pretrial incarceration, anxiety, and impairment of the defense itself. Applying these criteria to *Barker*, the Court concluded that despite the lengthy delay, Barker's defense was not prejudiced. He was on release throughout most of the period, and he failed seriously to assert the right to a speedy trial. *See also* FIFTH AMENDMENT, p. 201; SIXTH AMENDMENT, p. 241; SPEEDY TRIAL, p. 452.

*Significance*     *Barker v. Wingo* (407 U.S. 514: 1972) provides a unique two-edged protection in relation to a speedy trial. The defendant must

79

be protected from lengthy pretrial detention and diminution of the capacity to offer a defense, but the prosecutor's case must be similarly protected from erosion by delay. *Barker* established several criteria for assessing when a speedy trial has not occurred. In elucidating the four criteria listed, the Court rejected both the fixed time and "demand-waiver" approaches. Instead the Court opted for a balance test which was compatible with the Burger Court's general preference for examining the "totality of the circumstances." Three other cases speak to the matter of when the speedy trial protection begins, i.e., when the clock starts to run. *United States v. Marion* (404 U.S. 307: 1971) examined a three-year delay between a criminal act and the filing of charges. The Court concluded that the speedy trial guarantee does not apply "until the putative defendant in some way becomes an 'accused.'" *United States v. Lovasco* (431 U.S. 783: 1977) also considered preindictment delay. In *Lovasco* the prosecution had a chargeable case within a month of the crime but did not seek indictment for an additional 17 months. The delay was attributed to the inability to finish the investigation of the case against Lovasco as well as several others. Compounding the situation was the fact that the defendant lost the testimony of two witnesses who died during the delay. Nonetheless the Court found for the prosecution and refused to find an investigative delay prior to indictment a fatal defect. The Court refused to require prosecutors to charge as soon as evidence might be minimally sufficient. The Court did recognize that "reckless" preindictment delay or delay aimed at gaining an advantage did constitute a denial of due process. In *United States v. MacDonald* (456 U.S. 1: 1982), a murder case which drew national attention, the Court found that the time between dismissed charges brought within the military system of justice and the subsequent filing of civilian charges is not subject to speedy trial protection. The Court reiterated *MacDonald* in *United States v. Loud Hawk* (88 L.Ed. 2d 640: 1986), saying that the time when persons are free of all restrictions on their liberty is not to be included in the computation of delay. It is only the "actual restraints imposed by arrest and holding to answer a criminal charge that engages the protection of the Speedy Trial Clause." The Court also said in *Loud Hawk* that delay attributable to any interlocutory appeal must be weighed within the *Barker* test, but it does not necessarily weigh effectively toward the person invoking the Speedy Trial Clause. Thus the burden of demonstrating violation of the speedy trial protection clearly rests with the defense, and cases such as *Marion, Lovasco,* and *MacDonald* reflect the Court's preference for limiting the stages or time periods to which the speedy trial protection applies. In the meantime, Congress has legislated a speedy trial time period for federal courts. An accused must be brought to trial within 70 days of his or her first court appearance to answer criminal charges. That time period can be tolled for various reasons, usually consistent with defense requests. Some states have also enacted speedy trial legislation, frequently allowing six months from the time of arraignment. The balancing test of *Barker* still applies, however, especially to the states. On balance, for example, six months may or may not violate the *Barker* criteria.

## Confrontation

*Chambers v. Mississippi*, **410 U.S. 284, 93 S.Ct. 1038, 35 L.Ed. 2d 297 (1973)** Considered the effect of state rules of evidence on the exercise of the right of cross-examination. Defendant Chambers was charged with murder. He called a particular witness in order to introduce the witness' written confession to the crime. The witness repudiated his confession, at which point Chambers sought to cross-examine him as an adverse witness. The request was denied as well as other efforts to use the witness because of hearsay limitations and a state rule that a party may not impeach his or her own witness. With only Justice Rehnquist dissenting, the Supreme Court reversed Chambers' conviction. Justice Powell's opinion for the majority emphasized the "realities of the criminal process." Defendants must be able fully to explore testimony from all witnesses including their own because "in modern criminal trials defendants are rarely able to select their witnesses; they must take them where they find them." Impeaching his own witness may be crucial to a defendant's ability to put on a defense. In addition, such rules of evidence as the hearsay rule must allow exceptions and not "be applied mechanistically to defeat the ends of justice." Exception must occur where "constitutional rights directly affecting the ascertainment of guilt are implicated." Thus Chambers was deprived of his constitutional right of confrontation. *See also* CONFRONTATION, p. 397; *POINTER V. TEXAS* (380 U.S. 400: 1965), p. 247; SIXTH AMENDMENT, p. 241.

*Significance* *Chambers v. Mississippi* (410 U.S. 284: 1973) clearly reflects the view that a trial is a productive fact-finding process only if reliable evidence can be fully considered. The confrontation clause is designed to ensure evidence reliability by providing for cross-examination and requiring a witness to testify under oath. Further, the testimony of witnesses in open court can be assessed in terms of the witness' behavior or manner. The confrontation clause entitles a defendant to examine and perhaps challenge the full range of evidence against him or her in an attempt to develop the best factual defense. As seen in *Chambers*, the Burger Court was generally unreceptive to attempts to limit the examination/cross-examination process. *Chambers* is another Fourteenth Amendment extension of a federally protected right to the states. The Court held that the due process right found in the Fourteenth Amendment included the Sixth Amendment right to confront and cross-examine witnesses. In *Davis v. Alaska* (415 U.S. 308: 1974), the Court applied the *Chambers* decision to a case where a defendant had been denied the opportunity to disclose and develop during cross-examination the juvenile record of a crucial prosecution witness. While disclosure of the witness' status as a juvenile delinquent would conflict with the state's policy of preserving confidentiality of juvenile proceedings, a seven-member majority decided that disclosure of the witness' status was necessary to impeach the credibility of the witness. There are practical limits, however. In *Ohio v. Roberts* (448 U.S. 56: 1980), the Court returned to a variation of the *Pointer* fact situation. A witness after testifying at a preliminary hearing did not appear at the trial despite several subpoenas. A state statute permitted use of pre-liminary hearing testimony of a witness who could not be produced at the trial. The defendant objected to the use of the transcript despite the fact the witness had originally been called by the defense, since her preliminary hearing testimony had not been entirely favorable to his defense. The Supreme Court concluded that a sufficient good-faith effort had been made to locate the witness and that the prior testimony bore "sufficient indicia of reliability" to be used under these circum-stances. In *United States v. Inadi* (89 L.Ed. 2d 390: 1986), the Court examined preconditions for use of out-of-court statements in a trial where a witness fails to appear. It said the Confrontation Clause does not require the prosecution to make an actual showing that a nontes-tifying coconspirator is unavailable to testify if the prior statements otherwise satisfy rules governing coconspirator declarations. A dif-ferent confrontation issue was addressed in *Delaware v. Fensterer* (88 L.Ed. 2d 15: 1985). Here an expert witness for the prosecution was unable to recall the basis for an opinion he offered in testimony. The Court said this did not violate the defendant's right to confront the witness. The right to cross-examine is not denied "whenever the wit-ness' lapse of memory impedes one method of discrediting him." The Confrontation Clause includes no guarantee that every witness "will refrain from giving testimony that is marred by forgetfulness, confu-sion, or evasion." To the contrary, the requirements of the clause are generally satisfied when the defense has a full and fair opportunity to probe and expose these infirmities through cross-examination.

## Jury Selection

***Batson v. Kentucky*, 476 U.S. 000, 106 S.Ct. 1712, 90 L.Ed. 2d 69 (1986)** Held that the Equal Protection Clause precludes racially discriminatory use of peremptory challenges of potential jurors by prosecutors. During Batson's burglary trial, the prosecutor used his peremptory challenges to remove all four black persons from the venire. Batson was subsequently convicted by an all-white jury. The Kentucky Supreme Court affirmed the conviction based on *Swain v. Alabama* (380 U.S. 202: 1965). The Supreme Court used the *Batson* case to reexamine the element of *Swain* dealing with the burden of evidence a defendant must demonstrate in support of any claim of discriminatory use of peremptory challenges. In a 7–2 decision, the Court shifted much of the burden previously resting with the defendant to the prosecution. As established in previous cases, the Court reaffirmed that exclusion of blacks from jury service was an evil the Fourteenth Amendment was designed to cure. Purposeful racial discrimination violates a defendant's right to equal protection because it denies him or her the protection that trial by jury is intended to secure. A defendant is entitled to a venire of jurors that are indifferently chosen. Beyond its impact on defendants, the Court observed that such discrimination unlawfully denies persons an opportunity to participate in jury service and "undermines public confidence in the fairness of our system of justice." The targeted component of the selection process in this case was the peremptory challenge. Prosecutors are generally entitled to strike jurors for "any reason at all," although challenge exclusively on racial grounds is forbidden. Under *Swain,* the defendant was required to demonstrate an ongoing pattern of discrimination in order to set aside a conviction. The Court in *Batson* viewed this requirement as a "crippling burden of proof," and one which left prosecutorial strikes "largely immune from constitutional scrutiny." Accordingly, the Court concluded that a defendant may establish a *prima facie* case of intentional discrimination based exclusively on a prosecutor's use of the peremptory challenges at the defendant's trial. Once a defendant establishes such a *prima facie* case, the burden shifts to the state to offer a neutral explanation for challenging black jurors. The explanation need not rise to the level justifying exercise of a challenge for cause. The Court reiterated its recognition that the peremptory challenge "occupies an important position in our trial procedures." At the same time, the practice has been used as a means of discrimination. By requiring trial courts to be sensitive to discriminatory use of the procedure, *Batson* "enforces the mandate of equal protection and furthers the ends of justice." Justice Marshall would have gone further. Citing "common and flagrant" abuses of the peremptory challenge, he urged elimination of this step from the jury selection process. Chief Justice Burger and Justice Rehnquist dissented, voicing a preference for the evidentiary standard established in *Swain. See also:* RISTAINO V. ROSS (424 U.S. 589: 1976), p. 254; SIXTH AMENDMENT, p. 241.

*Significance*     *Batson v. Kentucky* (90 L.Ed. 2d 69: 1986) has its origin in *Norris v. Alabama* (294 U.S. 587: 1935). The *Norris* case, an appeal growing out of the notorious Scottsboro trial, prohibited systematic exclusion of persons from jury service on the basis of race. *Norris* allowed discriminatory practice to be inferred from statistics demonstrating inequity of access. Thirty years later, the Court first examined the use of peremptory strikes against claims of purposeful discrimination in *Swain v. Alabama* (380 U.S. 202: 1965). *Swain* was brought to the Supreme Court because more subtle methods of discrimination had been designed since *Norris* to minimize the involvement of blacks and others in jury service. The Court's decision in *Swain* did not abandon the basic thrust of *Norris* in terms of systematic exclusion, but it made the burden of proving discriminatory practice much more difficult. Though less compelling facts than were present in *Swain* have prevailed in establishing a *prima facie* case of discrimination in more recent cases, there remains no specific expectation that general population ratios will be reflected in specific juries. Cases such as *Taylor v. Louisiana* (419 U.S. 522: 1975) and *Duren v. Missouri* (439 U.S. 357: 1979) rejected certain state selection methods on the grounds that they systematically excluded women from jury service. But the Court has continued generally to defer to the states in the establishment and administration of techniques designed to draw juries and assure that they are a representative cross section of the community. In *Batson,* however, the Court for the first time imposed restraints on the way prosecutors may use their peremptory challenges. In doing so it substantially modified *Swain.* Where systematic racial exclusion can be shown, convictions must be reversed. The rule extends to intentional discrimination in the selection of grand jurors. Such discrimination is a "grave constitutional trespass" and wholly within the power of the state to prevent. Indictments stemming from defectively selected grand juries must bring about reversal of any subsequent convictions. The Court reaffirmed this principle in *Vasquez v. Hillary* (88 L.Ed. 2d 598: 1986), saying that even if the grand jury's action is "confirmed in hindsight" by a conviction on the indicted offense, the confirmation "does not suggest that discrimination did not impermissibly infect the framing of the indictment and, consequently, the nature or existence of the proceedings to come." A conviction simply cannot be "understood to cure the taint attributable to a charging body selected on the basis of race."

## Jury Selection

*Lockhart v. McCree*, **476 U.S. 000, 106 S.Ct. 1758, 90 L.Ed. 2d 137 (1986)**     Decreed that opponents of capital punishment may be excluded from juries in death penalty cases. McCree was tried for capital felony murder in a state proceeding. During the *voir dire* process, the judge removed for cause, prior to the guilt adjudication phase of a two-stage capital trial, all prospective jurors who indicated they could not impose the death penalty. A jury subsequently convicted McCree but rejected the death penalty at the sentencing stage. Instead it set punishment at life imprisonment without parole. McCree failed in his attempt for relief in the state courts and sought federal *habeas corpus* relief. He contended that the "death qualification" of the jurors remaining to determine his guilt or innocence deprived him of an impartial jury chosen from a representative cross section of the community. A federal district court ruled for McCree, a decision affirmed by the court of appeals. The Supreme Court reversed in a 6–3 vote. Justice Rehnquist began the majority opinion by pointing out several flaws in the evidence used by the lower courts to find that the death qualification produces conviction-prone juries. Even if the proposition could be demonstrated, Rehnquist said, the Constitution does not preclude use of death-qualified juries in capital trials. The fair cross-section requirement cannot be applied to limit use of either for cause or peremptory challenges or to require that petit juries (as distinct from jury panels or venires) reflect composition of the community at large. Further, the essence of a fair cross-section claim is the systematic exclusion of a distinctive group in the community. Groups defined solely in terms of shared attitudes which would substantially impair their functioning as jurors are not distinctive groups for fair cross-section purposes. Exclusion here did not occur for reasons completely unrelated to the ability of members of the group to function as jurors. This differentiated the *Lockhart* case from those where exclusion of a distinctive group arbitrarily skewed the composition of a jury and denied defendants the benefit of community judgment. In addition, exclusion in this case was on the basis of an attribute that is within the individual's control, unlike cases involving race, gender, or national origin. The Court also rejected McCree's contention that death qualification detracted from the impartiality of the jury and slanted the jury toward conviction. Rehnquist termed McCree's view of impartiality both illogical and hopelessly impractical. Had no death-qualifying questions been posed, the normal selection process could have produced the same jury which convicted McCree. Rehnquist also said the impartiality requirement cannot be read to require a certain mix of individual viewpoints. If such a requirement existed, trial judges would have to undertake the Sisyphean task of balancing juries, making sure that each was properly represented by Democrats and Republicans, young persons and old persons, white-collar executives and blue-collar laborers, and so on. Justices Marshall, Brennan, and Stevens dissented. Marshall said the decision provides the state with special advantage in cases where the punishment may be most severe. He maintained that the state's mere announcement that it is seeking the death penalty gives the prosecution license to empanel a jury especially likely to return a guilty verdict. *See also* RISTAINO V. ROSS (424 U.S. 589: 1976), p. 254; SIXTH AMENDMENT, p. 241.

*Significance*     *Lockhart v. McCree* (90 L.Ed. 2d 137: 1986) is the most recent of a series of decisions dealing with the troublesome issue of juror impartiality in capital cases. In *Witherspoon v. Illinois* (391 U.S. 510: 1968), the Court found that a jury cannot be selected which is uncommonly willing to condemn a person to death. Yet the Court refused to announce a per se constitutional rule requiring the reversal of every jury selected in the Illinois fashion. The Court said simply that in this case the jury "fell woefully short of that impartiality to which petitioner was entitled under the Sixth and Fourteenth Amendments." Writing for the majority, Justice Stewart found it clear that imposing the death penalty by a "hanging jury" would deprive the defendant of his life without due process of law. *Witherspoon,* however, was decided before the states were required to use two-stage processes separately to adjudicate guilt and then consider sentence. Since 1976, opponents of the death penalty have typically been excluded from both stages. This produced several follow-up cases to *Witherspoon.* While the latter remains generally in effect, the modifications brought in later cases up through *Lockhart* stem from the bifurcation requirement. In *Davis v. Georgia* (429 U.S. 122: 1976) the Court voided the death sentence of a state prisoner whose sentence had been imposed by a jury from which one prospective juror had been excluded because of general reservations about the death penalty. In *Adams v. Texas* (448 U.S. 38: 1980) the Court considered whether a state could exclude from a jury those persons unable to swear under oath that the extant possibility of the death penalty would not affect their deliberations. With only Justice Rehnquist dissenting, the Court decided that *Witherspoon* required reversal of the oath process. While still allowing exclusion of people who cannot be impartial, the majority was not satisfied that irrevocable opposition could be inferred from failure to swear to the impossibility of imposing the death penalty. The *Witherspoon* test for exclusion established that jurors could be excluded for cause only if they make it unmistakably clear they would automatically vote against the death penalty without regard to evidence. The Court softened this standard in *Wainwright v. Witt* (469 U.S. 412: 1985), where it held that a better criterion was whether a prospective juror's views would prevent or substantially impair performance of the juror function. *Wainwright* modified the *Witherspoon* automatic judgment language to say that in order to exclude for cause, a juror's bias need not be shown with unmistakable clarity. *Lockhart* clearly moved even further from *Witherspoon* in the direction of allowing a death qualification for prospective jurors.

## Jury Selection

*Ristaino v. Ross*, **424 U.S. 589, 96 S.Ct. 1017, 47 L.Ed. 2d 258 (1976)**    Considered the question of whether a defendant is constitutionally entitled to ask questions specifically directed toward racial prejudice during the *voir dire* examination of prospective jurors. The trial judge denied the defendant's motion to pose the question, and a black defendant was subsequently convicted in a state court of violent crimes against a white victim. The Supreme Court concurred in the trial judge's decision in a 6–2 vote. Justice Stevens did not participate. Justice Powell reasoned for the majority that the Constitution "does not always entitle a defendant to have questions posed during *voir dire* specifically directed to matters that conceivably might prejudice veniremen against him." Though circumstances might warrant specific questions about racial prejudice, these were matters to be handled through the exercise of "sound discretion" by the trial court, a function "particularly within the province of the trial judge." The mere fact that the victim and the defendant were of different races was not in itself something which was "likely to distort the trial." Therefore the defendant was not entitled to *voir dire* questions pursuing race prejudice. Justices Brennan and Marshall dissented. *See also* SIXTH AMENDMENT, p. 241.

*Significance*    *Ristaino v. Ross* (424 U.S. 589: 1976) is representative of the Burger Court's view of what kinds of questions a defendant is entitled to pursue during a *voir dire* examination. The *voir dire* process refers to a series of questions posed to prospective jurors to determine their impartiality. A prospective juror found to be partial on the basis of his or her responses is excused from service on a given jury "for cause." The supervision of *voir dire* rests with the trial judge. *Ristaino* decided that a trial judge's discretion has been properly exercised when a defendant is denied the opportunity to probe the racial prejudice of prospective jurors simply because the defendant and victim of the crime are of different races. *Ristaino* underscored the requirement that a defendant must demonstrate unusual circumstances such as the presence of a racial issue as an actual component of a particular case. A similar holding involving national origin was made in *Rosales-Lopez v. United States* (451 U.S. 182: 1981) in which a Mexican defendant, on trial for illegally bringing Mexican aliens into the country, wished to ask potential jurors about possible prejudice toward Mexicans. In *Ham v. South Carolina* (409 U.S. 524: 1973) the Court concluded that questions relating to racial prejudice *were* appropriate given the defendant's visibility in the civil rights movement in the locality of his trial. *Ristaino, Ham,* and *Rosales-Lopez* place the monitoring of the jury selection process, specifically the conduct of the *voir dire* examination, exclusively in the hands of the trial judge. This rule was modified for capital cases in *Turner v. Murray* (90 L.Ed. 2d 27: 1986). The Court said a capital defendant accused of an interracial crime is entitled to have prospective jurors informed of the race of the victim and questioned on the issue of racial bias during *voir dire*. The Court believed the risk of racial prejudice infecting a capital sentencing proceeding is especially serious in light of the complete finality of the death sentence. The Court has also held that a juror's failure to answer a question properly during *voir dire* does not require retrial. In *McDonough Power Equipment, Inc. v. Greenwood* (464 U.S. 548: 1984), the Court said that unless a showing can be made that failure to disclose actually denied a party an impartial jury, the invalidation of a jury decision is not required. To mandate vacating the jury decision in such a circumstance "ill serves the important end of finality." It would be "to insist on something closer to perfection than our judicial system can be expected to give."

## Pretrial Publicity

*Sheppard v. Maxwell*, **384 U.S. 33, 86 S.Ct. 1507, 16 L.Ed. 2d 600 (1966)**     Considered whether pervasive pretrial publicity, most of which was highly adverse to the defendant, deprived him of the fair trial mandated by the Sixth Amendment. Every stage of the *Sheppard* case was subjected to intensive media coverage, from inquest through indictment to the trial itself. The general substance of the coverage given Sheppard was hostile. Jurors were subjected to continuous publicity. Sheppard was eventually convicted of the murder of his wife, but the Supreme Court reversed the conviction with only Justice Black dissenting. The Court focused its discussion on the failures of the trial judge to adequately provide Sheppard with the "judicial serenity and calm to which he was entitled." Specifically, the trial judge should have (1) used stricter rules governing media use of the courtroom; (2) better insulated the witnesses from media representation; (3) limited the flow of information to the media from principals in the case; and (4) admonished the media to monitor the accuracy of their reports. The Court found the failure to insulate the jury properly the most glaring error in the trial. Several jurors admitted hearing media broadcasts about the case while serving. The Court said Sheppard's trial turned into an avoidable "carnival," and deprived Sheppard of the fair trial to which he was entitled. *See also* CHANDLER V. FLORIDA (449 U.S. 560: 1981), p. 262; GANNETT COMPANY V. DEPASQUALE (443 U.S. 368: 1979), p. 260; NEBRASKA PRESS ASSOCIATION V. STUART (427 U.S. 539: 1976), p. 259.

*Significance*    *Sheppard v. Maxwell* (384 U.S. 33: 1966) focused on the tension existing between a defendant's right to a fair trial and the First Amendment right of a free press. The press has always had the potential to impact negatively the fairness of criminal proceedings, but technical developments in the broadcast media have increased that potential dramatically. Virtually an entire community can be reached with information which may have a prejudicial effect on a particular case. The *Sheppard* case portrays these prejudicial effects at their worst. The result was that the Court did not require Sheppard to identify any *actual* prejudice against him. Since the totality of the circumstances raised the *possibility* of prejudice, that was sufficient to grant him relief. Even with the excesses that occurred in *Sheppard*, the Court resisted restricting the press. Instead the Court focused on the trial judge as the key figure in ensuring a fair trial. It talked about the option of delaying a trial until publicity had subsided or of changing the venue of a case. It emphasized how the *voir dire* examination could have been used to determine whether or not prejudicial publicity existed. It suggested sequestering or isolating juries in particularly visible cases. The caution of the Court in addressing press behavior prompted initiatives elsewhere. The industry itself, through meetings with representatives of trial courts, began to fashion principles of conduct for criminal case coverage. Much of the press now voluntarily complies. A subsequent decision, *Murphy v. Florida* (421 U.S. 794: 1975), provided more clarity on the question of when reported information becomes prejudicial. The Court said in *Murphy* that prospective jurors need not be "totally ignorant" of a case. They need only be able to "reach a verdict based on the evidence presented in the court." The thrust of *Murphy* was reiterated in *Patton v. Yount* (467 U.S. 1025: 1984), in which the defendant challenged the jury selection process for a retrial following his successful appeal. While extensive publicity had attended the first trial, the Court felt that the four-year period between trials had greatly reduced "any presumption of prejudice" that existed at the time of the initial trial. The Court said that when the matter of prejudice was examined, the relevant question was not whether the community remembered the case, but whether the jurors had such fixed opinions that they could not judge impartially. Press treatment of a case, especially one governed by self-imposed limits, does not necessarily mean the publicity is either prejudicial or adverse. The *Sheppard* case, however, clearly demonstrated the need for certain safeguards to ensure a fair trial for criminal defendants. The Court considered a different kind of threat to fair trial in *Holbrook v. Flynn* (89 L.Ed. 2d 525: 1986). In this case, a state court's security force was supplemented by four uniformed state troopers who sat in the first row of the courtroom spectator section during the trial. A unanimous Court ruled that the troopers' presence was not so inherently prejudicial as to deny the defendant a fair trial. Whenever a courtroom arrangement is challenged as inherently prejudicial, the issue is not whether the jurors articulated a consciousness of some prejudicial effect, but whether there was an unacceptable risk of prejudice. No such level of risk was found in *Holbrook*. Even if the jurors were aware that this deployment of troopers was not ordinary practice, the Court concluded that there was no reason to believe the troopers' presence tended to brand the defendant with guilt.

## Pretrial Publicity

***Nebraska Press Association v. Stuart*, 427 U.S. 530, 96 S.Ct. 2791, 49 L.Ed. 2d 683 (1976)** Examined the propriety of a "gag order" on the media as a way of preventing prejudicial pretrial publicity in violation of the fair trial requirement of the Sixth Amendment. *Sheppard v. Maxwell* (384 U.S. 33: 1966) placed the responsibility for maintaining a fair trial environment with the trial judge. In this case Judge Stuart restrained the media from "publishing or broadcasting accounts of confessions or admissions made by the accused or facts 'strongly implicative' of the accused" until such time as a jury was impaneled. The crime itself was the murder of six persons. Compliance with the order, as modified by the Nebraska Supreme Court, was achieved. The Supreme Court reviewed the case even though the order had expired by the time the case was argued. The Court unanimously rejected the gag order, noting also that the trial judge "acted responsibly, out of a legitimate concern, in an effort to protect the defendant's right to a fair trial." Nonetheless the Court viewed the restraining order as excessive. It suggested that truly extraordinary prejudicial publicity must be present in order to consider an action as severe as restraint. Given that the gag is a denial of free speech, the Court said it must review carefully whether the record justifies such an "extraordinary remedy." Included in such an examination are certain factors: (1) the "nature and extent" of the coverage; (2) alternative measures and their likely impact on mitigating publicity; and (3) the effectiveness of the gag order in preventing damaging and prejudicial publicity. The Court concluded that the record was not sufficient on the last two factors in this instance. Although the Court did not rule out the possibility that a restraining order might be sustained under certain circumstances, Judge Stuart's order was found to be excessive and a denial of the Nebraska Press Association's First Amendment rights. *See also* CHANDLER V. FLORIDA (449 U.S. 560: 1981), p. 262; GANNETT COMPANY V. DEPASQUALE (443 U.S. 368: 1979), p. 260; SHEPPARD V. MAXWELL (384 U.S. 33: 1966), p. 258.

*Significance*    *Nebraska Press Association v. Stuart* (427 U.S. 530: 1976) dealt with whether or not the press should be precluded from publishing what it already knows. This is a different problem from *Sheppard v. Maxwell* (384 U.S. 33: 1966), which focused on remedies *after* prejudicial pretrial publicity had already occurred. *Stuart* looked at the gag order as a means of stemming pretrial publicity *before* the fact. The prior restraint considerations of *Stuart* had been suspect for 25 years before the case was decided. While *Stuart* stopped short of invalidating the gag rule altogether, the clear thrust of the decision was to impose conditions which are virtually impossible to satisfy. The case then becomes a kind of intermediate point between a policy course stressing after-the-fact remedies and an approach that would close judicial proceedings to the public and the press. It is apparent from *Stuart* that prohibiting the press from reporting what they observe directly in open court is the least favored approach. The Court did uphold a protective order issued against publication of all information obtained through the discovery process in the defamation case of *Seattle Times Company v. Rhinehart* (464 U.S. 812: 1984). The Court said that limits on dissemination of information prior to trial implicates press protections "to a far lesser extent than would restraints in other contexts." The Court referred to rules authorizing discovery as "a matter of legislative grace," and said that a litigant has no First Amendment right to access information made available only for purposes of trying his or her suit. Restraints on discovered information are not limits on a traditionally public source of information.

## Pretrial Proceedings

***Gannett Company v. DePasquale*, 443 U.S. 368, 99 S.Ct. 2898, 61 L.Ed. 2d 608 (1979)**    Posed the question of whether or not the media could be denied access to a pretrial suppression hearing. If the press is allowed to observe a judicial proceeding, it generally will be allowed to report what it observed. Since both the defense and prosecution agreed to close the proceeding at issue in *Gannett*, the case really asked if the public has an independent right to an open pretrial judicial hearing. In a 5–4 decision, the Court upheld the closed hearing. The majority reasoned that pretrial suppression hearings as distinct from trials pose "special risks of unfairness." The objective of such hearings is to screen out unreliable or illegally obtained evidence. Pretrial publicity about such evidence could "influence public opinion" and "inform potential jurors of inculpatory information wholly inadmissible at the actual trial." As for the public's independent right to access, the Court stressed two points. First, public interest in the application of the Sixth Amendment does not create "a constitutional right on the part of the public." The public interest is protected by the participants in the adversary process. Thus the public has no claim that could displace the defendant's desire to close the proceeding. Second, the common law tradition recognizes the difference between a pretrial proceeding and the trial itself. "Pre-trial proceedings, precisely because of [a] concern for a fair trial, were never characterized by the degree of openness as were actual trials." Justices Blackmun, Brennan, Marshall, and White dissented. They concentrated on the benefits of open processes and what they considered to be unconstitutional limitations on the press. Justice Blackmun said that casting fair trial rights in terms of the accused is "not sufficient to permit the inference that the accused may compel a private proceeding simply by waiving that right." In addition, open proceedings are educative, allow police and prosecutorial performances to be scrutinized, and protect both the public and the defendant from partiality. The appearance of justice is important. "Secret hearings—though they are scrupulously fair in reality—are suspect by nature." *See also* CHANDLER V. FLORIDA (449 U.S. 560: 1981), p. 262; NEBRASKA PRESS ASSOCIATION V. STUART (427 U.S. 539: 1976), p. 259; SHEPPARD V. MAXWELL (384 U.S. 33: 1966), p. 258.

*Significance*     *Gannett Company v. DePasquale* (443 U.S. 368: 1979) sidesteps the censorship question raised in *Nebraska Press Association v. Stuart* (427 U.S. 539: 1976). The press was not prohibited from publishing information it already possessed in the *Gannett* case. Rather than consider infringement of the First Amendment rights of a free press, *Gannett* focused on whether or not a defendant's interest in closing a pretrial hearing supersedes the public's interest in an open proceeding. The decision clearly raised the prospect of all judicial proceedings, even trials, being closed at the initiative of the defense. The Court refused to take that step in *Richmond Newspapers, Inc. v. Commonwealth of Virginia* (448 U.S. 555: 1980). In *Richmond* the Court would not permit closure of trial to the public and media despite the defendant's request that this be done. With only Justice Rehnquist dissenting, the Court held that trials could not "summarily close courtroom doors" without interfering with First Amendment protections. Thus the potential for closure begun in *Gannett* was checked in *Richmond.* Remaining from *Gannett,* however, and reinforced by *Richmond,* is a great deference to trial judge discretion in dealing with closure. *Richmond* makes clear that closing trials is extreme, but if some overriding and demonstrable defendant interest can be shown, they may indeed be closed to the public and the press. What if a *defendant* wishes a pretrial proceeding to remain open? In *Waller v. Georgia* (467 U.S. 39: 1984), the Court held unanimously that the right to a public trial applies to a pretrial suppression hearing. The closure of such a hearing over the objections of a defendant can only occur if four criteria are met. First, the party wishing to close the proceeding must "advance an overriding interest that is likely to be prejudiced." Second, the closure must be "no broader than is necessary to protect that interest." Third, the trial court must consider "reasonable alternatives to closure." And finally, the trial court must make findings "adequate to support the closure."

## Assistance of Counsel

*Argersinger v. Hamlin,* **407 U.S. 25, 92 S.Ct. 2006, 32 L.Ed. 2d 530 (1972)** Extended to misdemeanors the *Gideon* doctrine that defendants in felony cases must be provided with a lawyer if they are indigent. *Gideon v. Wainwright* (372 U.S. 335: 1963) required that all indigent felony defendants be provided counsel at state expense. Argersinger was convicted of an offense punishable by up to six months imprisonment. He was indigent and unrepresented by counsel. In a unanimous decision the Supreme Court found his trial and conviction to be constitutionally defective. The opinion of the Court stresses these points: (1) the Court found nothing historically to indicate Sixth Amendment rights should be retractable in cases involving petty offenses; (2) the nature of the legal issues of a case should be the criterion for assessing necessity of counsel. Cases where lesser terms of imprisonment result may not be any less complex than cases where lengthy sentences may occur. (3) Given the assembly-line character of misdemeanor proceedings, assistance of counsel may be especially important. The basic holding of *Argersinger* is that absent a "knowing and intelligent waiver," no defendant may receive jail or prison time unless the defendant was represented by counsel at his or her trial. Several members of the Court wrote concurring opinions addressing the decision's implementation problems, but the basic holding was unanimous and included all four appointees of President Nixon. *See also* GIDEON V. WAINWRIGHT (372 U.S. 335: 1963), p. 264; POWELL V. ALABAMA

(287 U.S. 45: 1932), p. 263; *UNITED STATES V. WADE* (388 U.S. 218: 1967), p. 267.

*Significance*     *Argersinger v. Hamlin* (407 U.S. 25: 1972) reveals stress stemming from implementation and operational considerations. On the one hand the Court wished to extend *Gideon* and did so with fairly strong language. On the other hand the Court was faced with implementation of policy where the court system is most congested and where pressures for "assembly-line justice" are most acute. *Argersinger* was a compromise. It required counsel in misdemeanor cases, recognizing that the legal needs of defendants in these cases may be equal to or greater than defendants in felony cases. It also provided trial judges with the choice of not appointing counsel at all, although in refusing to do so the trial judge might forfeit imprisonment as a sentence option. Despite the problems in implementation, *Argersinger* has fundamentally altered the process of justice in misdemeanor courts, often called "city courts," "municipal courts," or "Justice of the Peace courts." It has also produced important legislation at the state and local level. Many cities, for example, now appoint or contract with counsel to provide legal assistance to persons who desire to try misdemeanor charges. Some states have decriminalized most traffic offenses in order to avoid the consequences of *Argersinger. Argersinger* was refined in *Scott v. Illinois* (440 U.S. 367: 1979), where the Supreme Court held that a state court does not have to appoint counsel where imprisonment is authorized for a particular offense but is not actually imposed. Together, *Argersinger* and *Scott* require greater caution by state and local governments in criminal proceedings. Many local judges are loath to imprison for misdemeanor convictions where counsel is not present, unless the defendant was made aware of his or her right to counsel before tendering a guilty plea. The *Scott* emphasis on actual incarceration was reinforced in *Lassiter v. Department of Social Services* (452 U.S. 18: 1981) where the Court held that counsel need not be provided to an indigent parent at a hearing that could terminate status as a parent. The Court said an indigent litigant was entitled to counsel only when the litigant is threatened with the deprivation of physical liberty. On a related matter, the Court held in *Ake v. Oklahoma* (470 U.S. 68: 1985) that an indigent defendant seeking to utilize the insanity defense is entitled to court-appointed psychiatric assistance. Justice Marshall wrote that a trial or sentencing proceeding is fundamentally unfair if the state proceeds against an indigent without insuring that he or she has access to advice that is "integral to the building of an effective defense." The impact of *Ake* is limited in that the great majority of states already provide such aid to indigent defendants.

## Effectiveness of Counsel

*Strickland v. Washington*, **466 U.S. 668, 104 S.Ct. 2052, 80 L.Ed. 2d 674 (1984)** Established a two-part test for examining the effectiveness of defense counsel. *Strickland v. Washington* developed from a death penalty sentencing proceeding which followed guilty pleas to three capital murder charges. During the plea colloquy, Washington claimed he had no significant prior record and that the crimes to which he was pleading were caused by extreme stress produced by his inability to provide for his family. Washington and his counsel discussed approaches to the sentencing hearing, and counsel decided that it was inadvisable to call character witnesses or seek psychiatric examination. The decision reflected counsel's judgment that Washington was better off using his plea colloquy as sufficient evidence on these points. The state would be unable to cross-examine Washington or introduce its own evidence as to his mental state. Counsel also chose not to request a presentence report because it would have shown Washington's prior record to be extensive. Nevertheless, the trial judge sentenced Washington to death. Washington appealed on grounds of ineffective counsel, citing counsel's failure to request a presentence report, seek psychiatric examination, and present character witnesses. In an 8–1 decision, the Court determined that Washington had been effectively represented. The opinion of the Court was written by Justice O'Connor who broadly sketched the context of the right to counsel, locating it in the Sixth Amendment which more generally addresses the concept of fair trial. O'Connor stated that at minimum a fair trial is one in which "evidence subject to adversarial testing is presented to an impartial tribunal for the resolution of defined issues." The benchmark for assessing a claim of ineffectiveness is "whether counsel's conduct so undermined the proper functioning of the adversarial process" that the proceeding cannot be relied upon as having produced a just result. Reversal on grounds of ineffective counsel requires the consideration of two elements: (1) that counsel performance is shown to be deficient, and (2) that the deficiency prejudiced the outcome. Counsel's representation must fall below an objective standard of reasonableness using prevailing professional norms. Judicial scrutiny of counsel performance should be highly deferential, avoiding the second-guessing of counsel judgment. The courts should indulge a strong presumption that counsel conduct falls within a wide range of reasonable professional assistance. Accordingly, strategic choices made after thorough investigation of plausible options are virtually unchallengeable. Despite the deference recommended, some cases require reversal because their result was prejudiced. The defendant must show that there is a reasonable probability that without the counsel's misrepresentation the result of the proceeding would have been different. Such a probability must be sufficient to undermine confidence in the outcome of the proceeding. Review of this issue must consider the totality of evidence entered at the proceeding. O'Connor concluded by saying a number of practical considerations are crucial to application of the standards she discussed. Most important in reviewing claims of ineffectiveness is that "the principles we have stated do not establish mechanical rules." The ultimate focus must be on the fundamental fairness of the proceeding. In examining Washington's case by these standards, the Court decided that had counsel offered the evidence Washington cited, it would "barely have altered" the profile on which the sentence was based. Justice Marshall dissented. He said the standards for effective counsel as defined here by the Court are so malleable they do not address the problem. *See also* ASSISTANCE OF COUNSEL, p. 399; GIDEON V. WAINWRIGHT (372 U.S. 335: 1963), p. 264.

*Significance*    *Strickland v. Washington* (466 U.S. 668: 1984) emphasized that the most important factor in assessing the effectiveness of counsel is whether or not the adversarial process is maintained. So long as counsel is "reasonably effective" and there is no "reasonable probability" of a different outcome, the quality of assistance is presumed adequate. The matter of counsel effectiveness has long been troublesome, with no precise standards in place for cases in which it is an issue. The most generally recognized criterion is the "mockery of justice" standard, but this criterion requires extraordinary ineffectiveness to be invoked. Another example of a case in which the Court rejected claims of ineffective assistance is *Jones v. Barnes* (463 U.S. 745: 1983). The Court held that counsel assigned to handle an appeal for a convicted defendant need not raise every issue suggested by the defendant. For courts to "second-guess reasonable professional judgments and impose on appointed counsel a duty to raise every 'colorable' claim suggested by a client" would not well serve the goal of vigorous and effective advocacy. In *United States v. Cronic* (466 U.S. 648: 1984), the Court ruled that in assessing whether there had been a breakdown of the adversarial process, a court may not conclude by inference that circumstances surrounding representation constitute denial of effective assistance. Two years later, in *Nix v. Whiteside* (89 L.Ed. 2d 123: 1986), the Court unanimously ruled that an attorney does not deny a client effective assistance by insisting that the client testify truthfully. At a point where the client indicated an intention to perjure himself at his trial, the attorney threatened to inform the trial court and withdraw as counsel. The Court said the attorney's duty to the client's cause is limited to "legitimate, lawful conduct compatible with the truth-seeking objective of a trial." The right to testify does not extend to testifying falsely, and the right to counsel "includes no right to have a lawyer who will cooperate with planned perjury." Finally, in *Evitts v. Lucey* (469 U.S. 387: 1985), the Court added that effectiveness standards apply to a first appeal as well as to the trial stage of a criminal proceeding.

## Self-Representation

*Faretta v. California,* **422 U.S. 806, 95 S.Ct. 2525, 45 L.Ed. 2d 562 (1975)**     Considered whether or not a state criminal defendant's defense of himself met the Sixth Amendment requirement of assistance of counsel. By the mid-1970s it was clearly established that a person being tried on a criminal charge in either a state or federal court must be afforded the right of assistance of counsel. A six-justice Supreme Court majority held that Faretta could constitutionally assist and defend himself. The majority, through Justice Stewart, recognized that self-representation may be an unwise course for a criminal defendant, but the Court said it is "one thing to hold that every defendant, rich or poor, has the right to the assistance of counsel, and quite another to say that a State may compel a defendant to accept a lawyer he does not want." Free choice was crucial to the majority decision. The choice of a defense belongs to the defendant, including the question of counsel. Although the defendant's choice may be "ultimately to his own detriment, his choice must be honored." A trial judge must make the defendant "aware of the dangers and disadvantages of self-representation" so that the record can reflect that the defendant made a choice with "eyes open." The criterion by which the determination is to be made is not technical. It makes no difference "how well or poorly Faretta had mastered the intricacies of the hearsay rule and the California code provisions." The decision rested with his "knowing exercise of the right to defend himself." In the case appealed the majority concluded that Faretta had been denied a constitutional right to "conduct his own defense." Chief Justice Burger and Justices Blackmun and Rehnquist dissented. Burger could find no Sixth Amendment right to represent oneself. The "spirit and logic" of the amendment required that the accused receive "the fullest possible defense." He did not agree with the freedom of choice argument of the majority and opined that the trial court retains discretion to reject a waiver of counsel. The Chief Justice was concerned that greater congestion of the courts would follow *Faretta,* and that the quality of justice would suffer. Blackmun also found the Sixth Amendment to stop short of conveying a right of self-representation. He felt the decision would cause "procedural confusion without advancing any significant strategic interest of the defendant." *See also* GIDEON V. WAINWRIGHT (372 U.S. 335: 1963), p. 264; POWELL V. ALABAMA (287 U.S. 45: 1932), p. 263; SIXTH AMENDMENT, p. 241.

*Significance*     *Faretta v. California* established the rule that a defendant has a right to carry on his or her own defense without violating the "assistance of counsel" requirement of the Sixth Amendment. The case ran absolutely counter to many contemporary Supreme Court decisions that found "the guiding hand of counsel" to be indispensable to due process. *Faretta* not only recognizes the option of self-representation but accords it the status of a protected right on par with assistance of counsel. In addition *Faretta* holds that a defendant need not demonstrate even minimal levels of legal skill to exercise the right of self-representation. Like any other constitutional provision, the right to counsel may be waived voluntarily. More recently, the Court examined the issue of unsolicited participation by standby counsel as it relates to the right of self-representation. In *McKaskle v. Wiggins* (465 U.S. 168: 1984), the Court said that the categorical silencing of standby counsel is not required as long as the defendant is able to retain control over the conduct of his or her own defense. The Court said that to determine whether or not *Faretta* rights have been preserved, "the primary focus must be on whether the defendant had a fair chance to present his case in his own way." As long as the jury perceives that the defendant is representing himself, even overzealous participation by standby counsel need not be absolutely barred. *Faretta* also raises important questions about the quality of counsel. They are addressed in *Strickland v. Washington* (466 U.S. 668: 1984).

## Plea Bargaining

*Santobello v. New York*, **404 U.S. 257, 29 S.Ct. 495, 30 L.Ed. 2d 427 (1971)**     Considered the issue of what happens when the state fails to honor a commitment made during plea bargaining discussions. Santobello was indicted for two felonies and agreed to enter a guilty plea in exchange for no sentence recommendation by the prosecuting attorney. At the sentencing hearing, delayed twice at defendant's initiative, a new prosecuting attorney appeared. Apparently ignorant of his colleague's promise, the new prosecutor recommended the maximum sentence, which Santobello received. The trial judge said, however, he was not influenced by the prosecutor's recommendation. The Court concluded that Santobello's sentence must be vacated, although a minority of the Court (Justices Marshall, Brennan, and Stewart) argued that the defendant should be allowed to withdraw his guilty plea entirely. On the basic sentence question the Court said the condition of no sentence recommendation was an integral part of the bargain made with the prosecutor. The Court did not forgive the failure of one prosecutor to communicate the elements of the negotiation to his successor. The prosecutor's office has "the burden of 'letting the left hand know what the right hand is doing' or has done." The Court said further that "the breach of agreement was inadvertent," but that "does not lessen its impact." *Santobello* represented to the Court "another example of an unfortunate lapse in orderly prosecutorial procedures," presumably a product of excessively high caseloads. But while workload "may well explain these episodes, it does not excuse them." The plea process "must be attended by safeguards to insure the defendant what is reasonably due in the circumstances." The position of the Court was that where pleas "rest in any significant degree on a promise or agreement of the prosecutor, such promise must be fulfilled." *See also* BOYKIN V. ALABAMA (395 U.S. 238: 1969), p. 270; BRADY V. UNITED STATES (397 U.S. 742: 1970), p. 272; BORDENKIRCHER V. HAYES (434 U.S. 357: 1978), p. 275.

*Significance*     *Santobello v. New York* (404 U.S. 257: 1971) illustrates the problems attendant to a congested court system where over 90 percent of criminal cases are disposed of by means of the plea. The system requires nontrial dispositions in order to keep pace with case volume. Most cases are passed from one assistant prosecutor to another within a prosecutor's office as the next stage of the process is reached. The left hand does not always know what the right hand has done. Plea bargaining has long been a suspect practice anyway. The National Advisory Commission of Criminal Justice Standards and Goals strongly urged the abolition of plea bargaining in the early 1970s. *Santobello* addresses several important issues related to the Advisory Commission's recommendations. First, the Court established the basic expectation that where promises are instrumental in achieving a plea, the integrity of the bargaining process must be maintained and the promises honored. *Santobello* defines a performance standard for prosecutors. Second, *Santobello* permits a defendant in a criminal case to enforce a plea agreement against the government. Although *Santobello* involved only a prosecutorial recommendation, it raised the specter of a prosecutor offering to dismiss other counts against a defendant and not prosecuting for similar offenses within a given time. The lower courts have frequently invoked *Santobello* when a defendant alleges and proves a plea agreement has been violated. It is not uncommon for courts to dismiss criminal proceedings when prosecutorial authorities have reneged on a plea. This kind of specific enforcement may be the most important aspect of *Santobello*. Third, *Santobello* gave the Court an opportunity to speak generally to the status of plea bargaining. The

Court gave the practice a strong endorsement. It referred to plea bargaining as an "essential component of the administration of justice. Properly administered, it is to be encouraged." The Court itemized several reasons why plea bargaining should be regarded not only as essential but as "highly desirable." The advantages included finality, pretrial confinement, conservation of scarce resources, and enhancement of rehabilitative prospects. Taken with the positive language found in *Brady v. United States* (397 U.S. 742: 1970), the *Santobello* language and decision can be viewed as foreclosing the possibility that the Court will call for the abolition of plea bargaining in the near future. But *Santobello* does not create an absolute right to have a plea bargain enforced. In *Mabry v. Johnson* (467 U.S. 504: 1984) a defendant, following a successful appeal, accepted a plea proposal offered by the prosecutor rather than chance a retrial. The proposal was subsequently withdrawn on the ground that it had been mistakenly tendered. An alternative proposal was offered but rejected, and a new trial was held. After a mistrial was declared, the defendant accepted the second offer and was sentenced accordingly. The defendant then appealed again, arguing that the prosecutor was precluded from withdrawing the original offer once the defendant had accepted it. The Supreme Court disagreed unanimously. The Court said Johnson pled knowing what the prosecutor would recommend, he did so with the advice of competent counsel, and he was fully aware of the consequences. His plea was in no way the product of governmental deception. It did not rest on an unfulfilled promise, and it "fully satisfied the test for voluntariness and intelligence."

# 5. The Eighth Amendment

## Preventive Detention

***Schall v. Martin*, 467 U.S. 253, 104 S.Ct. 2403, 81 L.Ed. 2d 207 (1984)**     Upheld the preventive detention of juveniles. *Schall v. Martin* examined a state statute that authorized pretrial detention of a juvenile as long as it could be shown that there was "serious risk" of the juvenile committing additional crimes if released. Martin brought suit claiming the statute was unconstitutional on due process and equal protection grounds. A United States district court found the law in violation of the Due Process Clause and ordered the release of all juveniles detained under the statute. The Supreme Court reversed the district court in a 6–3 decision. The opinion of the Court was delivered by Justice Rehnquist. He said the question before the Court was whether or not preventive detention of juveniles is compatible with "fundamental fairness." To address this issue properly, the Court felt that answers to two inquiries were necessary: (1) is a legitimate state interest served by preventive detention; and (2) are the procedural safeguards adequate to authorize the pretrial detention. The Court determined that crime prevention is a "weighty social objective," and a state's legitimate and compelling interest in protecting its citizenry from crime "cannot be doubted." That interest "persists undiluted in the juvenile context." The harm caused by crime is not dependent upon the age of the perpetrator, and the harm to society may be even greater given the high rate of recidivism among juveniles. In addition, the juvenile's liberty interest may be subordinated to the state's "parens patriae interest in preserving and promoting the welfare of the child." Rehnquist argued that society has a legitimate interest in protecting a juvenile from the consequences of his or her criminal activity. This includes the potential injury that may occur when a victim resists and "the downward spiral of criminal activity into which peer pressure may lead the child" persists. The Court saw the state interest as substantial and legitimate, a view "confirmed by the widespread use and judicial acceptance of preventive detention for juveniles." Rehnquist observed that "mere invocation of a legitimate purpose" will not justify particular restrictions and conditions of confinement amounting to punishment.

The Court found the statute in question to have nonpunitive objectives, however. The detention specified was "strictly limited in time," and it entitled the juvenile to an expedited fact-finding hearing. The Court then addressed the procedural issue of whether there was "sufficient protection against erroneous and unnecessary deprivation of liberty." The Court found that the statute provided "far more predetention protection" than required for probable cause determinations for adults. While the initial appearance is informal, full notice is given and stenographic records are kept. The juvenile is accompanied by a parent or guardian and is informed of his or her constitutional rights, including the right to remain silent and be represented by counsel. Finally, the Court rejected the contention that the statute's standard for detention, serious risk of additional criminal conduct, was "fatally vague." Prediction of future criminal conduct is a judgment based on "a host of variables which cannot be readily codified." Nonetheless, the decision on detention is based on "as much information as can reasonably be obtained at the initial appearance," and is not impermissibly vague. Justices Marshall, Brennan, and Stevens dissented. They saw the statute as a violation of due process because it allowed punishment before final adjudication of guilt. They felt the crime prevention interest was insufficient justification for the infringement of the detainee's rights. *See also* BAIL, p. 387; DUE PROCESS CLAUSE, p. 405.

*Significance*     The Court's decision in *Schall v. Martin* (467 U.S. 253: 1984) was its first treatment of preventive detention. Prior to *Schall*, the Court had allowed preventive detention statutes to stand without review, silently agreeing with their view of pretrial release. While bail should have the effect of ensuring an appearance at subsequent proceedings, those persons released also constitute a continuing threat to society. The policy of preventive detention is aimed at confining defendants who present a serious threat of additional criminal conduct. Although such a policy may be effective as a crime prevention strategy, it also runs counter to the presumption of innocence. For many, it constitutes imposition of punishment before adjudication of guilt. *Schall* suggests that the Court may be receptive to preventive detention statutes for adult defendants as well as juveniles.

## Mandatory Death Penalty

*Woodson v. North Carolina*, **428 U.S. 280, 96 S.Ct. 2978, 49 L.Ed. 2d 944 (1976)**     Examined the adequacy of the mandatory death sentence. Several states responded to *Furman v. Georgia* (408 U.S. 238: 1972) with revisions in their capital punishment statutes making the death penalty mandatory for certain offenses. A five-justice Supreme Court majority held that the mandatory approach was "unduly harsh and unworkably rigid." The five said allowing some discretion in sentencing was more compatible with evolving standards of social decency, a frequently mentioned criterion in cruel and unusual punishment cases. The fact that juries possessing discretion infrequently impose capital punishment suggests that capital punishment is viewed as "inappropriate" in a large number of cases. A second defect cited by the majority was that mandatory sentences did not remedy *Furman* flaws. The mandatory approach "papers over" the problem of jury discretion. There are no standards by which to determine "which murderer shall live and which shall die." Neither does the mandatory approach allow a review of arbitrary death sentences. The third flaw in the mandatory approach was said to be its undifferentiating character. The statutes did not allow for the consideration of factors particular to the crime and the defendant. They precluded consideration of "compassion or mitigating factors." The statutes treated all convicted persons "as members of a faceless, undifferentiated mass to be subjected to the blind infliction of the penalty of death." The four dissenters, through Justice Rehnquist, were troubled by the majority's process focus. Justice Rehnquist felt the Court should confine itself to a simple determination of whether a punishment is cruel. The Court had already concluded in *Gregg v. Georgia* (428 U.S. 153: 1976) that capital punishment was not a cruel and unusual punishment per se. To invalidate the statute on procedural grounds was therefore inappropriate. *See also* COKER V. GEORGIA (433 U.S. 584: 1977), p. 298; EIGHTH AMENDMENT, p. 289; *FURMAN V. GEORGIA* (408 U.S. 238: 1972), p. 294; GREGG V. GEORGIA (428 U.S. 153: 1976), p. 295.

*Significance*    *Woodson v. North Carolina* (428 U.S. 280: 1976) gave the Court an opportunity to choose between two alternative approaches to capital punishment. *Woodson* clearly reflected the Court's preference for retaining some discretion with sentencers in capital cases. To implement capital punishment reasonably, the sentencer must evaluate the specific details of a particular case against criteria defined by state legislatures. The mandatory approach precludes consideration of the factors that may make a case unique. That is its fatal flaw. The Court has since underscored the inadequacy of the mandatory approach. In striking down a Louisiana statute which called for capital punishment for the deliberate killing of a firefighter or police officer, the Court said, "It is incorrect to suppose that no mitigating circumstances can exist when the victim is a police officer." Neither can the scope of sentencer considerations be improperly restricted. In *Lockett v. Ohio* (438 U.S. 586: 1978) the Court held that limiting a sentencer to a narrow range of possible mitigating circumstances was unsatisfactory. In *Eddings v. Oklahoma* (455 U.S. 104: 1982) the Court remanded the case of a 16-year-old boy sentenced to death by a trial judge who determined that, as a matter of state law, he could not consider as a mitigating circumstance the youth's "unhappy upbringing and emotional disturbance." And in *Skipper v. South Carolina* (90 L.Ed. 2d 1: 1986), the Court held that a state could not exclude introduction of certain testimony representing the defendant's record of good behavior while in jail from the jury making a determination of his sentence in a capital case. Using a rationale similar to that in *Lockett* and *Eddings*, the Court said the defendant's capacity to make a good adjustment to prison life reflected an aspect of his character relevant to the jury's sentencing decision. *Woodson* struck a middle ground between complete sentencer discretion and the complete mandating of the sentence of death. Is the mandating of sentences other than death not equally offensive to the Eighth Amendment? That question was left to other cases for resolution.

## Death Penalty: Proportionality

*Pulley v. Harris*, **465 U.S. 37, 104 S.Ct. 871, 79 L.Ed. 2d 29 (1984)**        Held that a state need not conduct a comparative proportionality review in capital punishment cases. While such comparative reviews are performed in a number of states, the Court ruled in *Pulley v. Harris* that the Eighth Amendment did not mandate such reviews. Harris was convicted of a capital crime and sentenced to death. He appealed to the California Supreme Court on the grounds that appellate review did not require a comparison of his sentence with sentences imposed in similar capital cases. Failing with the state courts, Harris sought *habeas corpus* relief in the federal courts. The United States Court of Appeals eventually ruled that the proportionality relief Harris sought was constitutionally required. In a 7–2 decision, the Supreme Court disagreed. The opinion of the Court was written by Justice White. He states that traditionally the concept of proportionality had been used in conjunction with "an abstract evaluation of the appropriateness of a sentence for a particular crime." This involved comparing the gravity of the offense and the severity of the penalty to determine if the punishment was disproportionate or excessive. In this case, however, the defendant sought review of a different sort. Harris asked the Court to consider whether his sentence was unacceptable because it was disproportionate to the punishment imposed on others convicted of the same crime. Harris argued that when the states redrafted their capital punishment laws after *Furman v. Georgia* (408 U.S.

238: 1972), most states required such a comparative review. The Court upheld some of the state capital punishment revisions, many of which did indeed require proportionality review. To find proportionality review constitutional does not mean that it is indispensable, however. To endorse these rewritten statutes as a whole is not to hold that anything different is unacceptable. *Gregg v. Georgia* (428 U.S. 153: 1976) is an example of the Court upholding a revised death penalty statute which included proportionality review. While such review as found in *Gregg* was considered an "additional safeguard against arbitrary or capricious sentencing," the Court did not see it as so critical that without the review the statute would not have passed constitutional muster. The Court concluded that there was no basis for saying that a proportionality review is required in every case. The Court also said that even if a death penalty sentencing process was "so lacking in other checks on arbitrariness" that it could not pass scrutiny without a comparative proportionality review, the California statute was not of that sort. Rather, it provided a sufficiently deliberative and structured consideration of the sentencing process as to be beyond challenge. Justices Brennan and Marshall dissented. They said that while it is no panacea, proportionality review "often serves to identify the most extreme examples of disproportionality among similarly situated defendants." In their opinion, such review serves to eliminate a portion of "the irrationality that currently infects imposition of the death penalty." *See also* CRUEL AND UNUSUAL PUNISHMENT, p. 401; *FURMAN V. GEORGIA* (408 U.S. 238: 1972), p. 294; *GREGG V. GEORGIA* (428 U.S. 153: 1976), p. 295.

*Significance*     The holding in *Pulley v. Harris* (465 U.S. 37: 1984) was that state courts are not required to perform a comparative proportionality review of death sentences. Following *Furman v. Georgia* (408 U.S. 238: 1972) 36 states undertook extensive revision of their capital punishment statutes. The Court subjected these revisions to careful scrutiny during the next decade and found procedural defects in some of them. Since 1983, however, the Court has seemed to be satisfied that the principal process questions have been adequately addressed. In *Pulley,* the Court acknowledged that comparative proportionality reviews may be a useful component of a capital punishment policy, but it refused to mandate the step. Similar deference to state sentencing procedures was shown in *Spaziano v. Florida* (468 U.S. 447: 1984), where the Court upheld a death sentence imposed by a judge following a jury's recommendation of a life sentence. The Court said that a defendant is not entitled to a jury determination of sentence. Neither is a jury's recommendation so final as to preclude override by the trial judge. Decisions such as *Pulley* and *Spaziano* indicate that the Court feels the death penalty statutes now in place satisfy all constitutional requirements. Although some nonuniform processes can be found state to state, the differences do not now constitute critical enough factors for the Court to interfere.

# 6. Equal Protection and Privacy

## Right of Privacy, 128

# RACIAL DISCRIMINATION
## Reverse Discrimination

*Regents of the University of California v. Bakke*, **438 U.S. 265, 98 S.Ct. 2733, 57 L.Ed. 2d 750 (1978)**    Rejected the use of quotas in university admissions procedures, but permitted the use of race as a factor in recruiting heterogeneous student bodies. *Regents of the University of California v. Bakke* represented the Supreme Court's first discussion of the merits of affirmative action. The troublesome question posed by affirmative action programs is whether or not preference may be extended to a particular racial or ethnic group in order to correct historical inequalities. Can certain intentional preferences constitutionally be permitted because of their compensatory character? The medical school at the University of California at Davis admitted 100 students annually. To assure minority representation within the student body, 16 places were reserved for minority applicants. Bakke, a white applicant, was twice denied admission although his credentials were better than some of the minority applicants admitted under the affirmative action policy. Bakke brought suit arguing that the racially sensitive quota system at Davis violated Title VI of the Civil Rights Act of 1964. The Act prohibited discrimination in programs receiving federal funding. The Court resolved the case by finding for both sides. In a 5–4 split, the Court ruled that the Davis quota system was impermissible and ordered that Bakke be admitted. At the same time, the Court also held in a 5–4 vote that a state university may take race into account in allowing for a diverse student body. Each issue split the Court into two blocs of four members each, with Justice Powell providing the decisive vote on each judgment. Justice Powell joined Chief Justice Burger and Justices Rehnquist, Stewart, and Stevens on the quota component, but aligned himself with Justices Brennan, Marshall, White, and Blackmun on the issue of limited affirmative action efforts. Justice Powell's opinion rejected the quota approach and the injustice of racial classifications generally. The Fourteenth Amendment confers protection to individuals, he said. The "guarantee of

111

equal protection cannot mean one thing when applied to one individual and something else when applied to a person of another color." Justice Powell rejected the view that race was not a suspect classification when applied to the white majority because the purpose of such classification was benign. Individuals within that class "are likely to find little comfort in the notion that the deprivation they are asked to endure is merely the price of membership in the dominant majority and that its imposition is inspired by the supposedly benign purpose of aiding others." Noting that the white majority itself was composed of various minority groups, Justice Powell feared that courts would forever be asked to assess the degree of discrimination each has suffered and the redress each was due. By "hitching the meaning of the Equal Protection Clause to these transitory considerations, we would be holding, as a constitutional principle, that judicial scrutiny of classifications touching on racial and ethnic background may vary with the ebb and flow of political forces." Justice Powell did, however, recognize attainment of a diverse student body as a constitutionally permissible goal for an institution of higher education. Indeed, he said the nation's future depends upon leaders trained through wide exposure, which comes through a diverse student body. He referred to the Harvard admissions program which assigns a plus to particular racial or ethnic backgrounds, but still treats each applicant as an individual in the admissions process. In striking the Davis quota system, the Court said it need not reach the broader constitutional question of race as a factor in admissions decisions. It was enough to say Title VI required Bakke's admission and the striking of Davis' reserved seat policy. A majority of the Court saw the Davis program as educationally sound and sufficiently important to justify the use of race-conscious admissions programs. The Davis approach did not "stigmatize any discrete group or individual," and thus was adequate as a means of remedying the effects of past societal discrimination. *See also* EQUAL PROTECTION CLAUSE, p. 313; *FULLILOVE V. KLUTZNICK* (448 U.S. 448: 1980), p. 339; *WASHINGTON V. DAVIS* (426 U.S. 229: 1976), p. 333.

*Significance*    *Regents of the University of California v. Bakke* (438 U.S. 265: 1978) was a compromise holding. While the Court rejected quotas as such, it still allowed universities to manipulate admissions to produce heterogeneous student bodies. The Court had an opportunity to deal with the reverse discrimination issue four years earlier in *DeFunis v. Odegaard* (416 U.S. 312: 1974). DeFunis argued that he had been denied admission to the University of Washington Law School because of a preferential admissions policy very much like that used at Davis. DeFunis, however, had been admitted to the law school under court order and was actually close to graduation at the time the case was presented to the Supreme Court. Five members of the Court decided the case was moot and avoided speaking to the equal protection question. Following *Bakke*, a more positive affirmative action decision came from the Court in *United Steelworkers of America v. Weber* (443 U.S. 193: 1979). The Court upheld a private and voluntary employee training program against a challenge under Title VII of the Civil Rights Act of 1964. The program gave selection preference to black employees for training, although not to the total exclusion of white employees. The Court held more recently in *Firefighters Local #1784 v. Stotts* (467 U.S. 561: 1984) that federal judges may not ignore seniority rights in order to protect newly hired minority employees from layoffs forced by budget reductions. In a 6–3 decision, the Court said that Title VII exempts seniority systems unless the system is shown to have been designed to discriminate purposefully.

## THE NEW EQUAL PROTECTION
### Tax Exempt Status

*Bob Jones University v. United States*, **461 U.S. 574, 103 S.Ct. 2017, 76 L.Ed. 2d 157 (1983)** Ruled that the federal government may revoke or deny tax exemptions to private educational institutions practicing racial discrimination. The heart of the dispute in *Bob Jones University v. United States* was an Internal Revenue Service (IRS) interpretation of two sections in the Internal Revenue Code. Section 501 (c)(3) allowed tax exemptions for institutions "organized and operated exclusively for religious, charitable, or educational purposes," while Section 170 granted charitable deductions for contributors to such institutions. In 1970 the IRS determined that the provisions could not apply to private schools engaged in racial discrimination. It issued a revenue ruling that such schools were no longer charitable institutions. Bob Jones University admitted black students but denied admission to applicants who were "known to advocate" interracial marriage or dating or were married to a person of a different race. The university said its discriminatory policies were justified because they were required by religious beliefs. The Supreme Court upheld the IRS determination to withdraw exempted status from Bob Jones in an 8–1 ruling. The university argued that as long as it remained either a religious or an educational institution, it need not also be charitable to qualify for the exemption. The Court responded through Chief Justice Burger by saying that Section 501 (c)(3) must be interpreted against the background of Congressional intent. The Court found "unmistakable evidence" that "entitlement to tax exemption depends on meeting certain common law standards of charity—namely, that an institution seeking tax exempt status must serve a public purpose and not be contrary to established public policy." The exempted institution "must demonstrably serve and be in harmony with the public interest," because all taxpayers are affected by exemptions or deductions granted by the government. Other taxpayers in effect become indirect or vicarious donors. The institution, therefore, cannot have objectives "so at odds with the common community conscience as to undermine any public benefit that might otherwise be conferred." As a result, racially discriminatory schools cannot be viewed as providing a benefit within the context of charitable or within Congressional intent underlying Sections 170 and 501 (c)(3). The Court's focus then turned to the authority of the IRS to make its ruling. Bob Jones argued that only Congress itself could alter the scope of the two sections. The Court disagreed. The chief justice noted that Congress refused to reverse the ruling despite numerous opportunities. Burger called the congressional nonaction significant and thought it hardly conceivable that Congress was not abundantly aware of what was going on. Similarly, public policy at the time of the ruling was unmistakably clear on the issue of racial discrimination. It would be "anomalous for the Executive, Legislative, and Judicial Branches to reach conclusions that add up to a firm public policy on racial discrimination, and at the same time have the IRS blissfully ignore what all three branches of the Federal Government had declared." Finally, the Court dismissed the argument that the discrimination was based on sincerely held religious beliefs. The chief justice wrote that religious liberty may be limited if the state is pursuing an overriding governmental interest. The interest in eliminating racial discrimination was seen as a fundamentally overriding interest that "substantially outweighs whatever burden denial of tax benefits places on petitioners' exercise of their religious beliefs." Justice Rehnquist dissented. While agreeing that national policy is opposed to racial discrimination and that Congress has the power to further that policy by denying tax exemptions, Justice Rehnquist felt that Congress had yet actually to do so. "Whatever the reasons for the failure, this Court should not legislate for Congress." See also EQUAL PROTECTION CLAUSE, p. 313; FIRST AMENDMENT, p. 77; FREE EXERCISE CLAUSE, p. 413.

*Significance*        The decision in *Bob Jones University v. United States* (461 U.S. 574: 1983) permits denial of tax exempt status to private educational institutions practicing racial discrimination even if such behavior is grounded in religious doctrine. The holding clearly subordinates the burden imposed on a religious institution through the loss of an exemption to the interest of eliminating racial discrimination. Previous to the *Bob Jones* case, the Court had ruled in *Norwood v. Harrison* (413 U.S. 455: 1973) that state-purchased textbooks could not be loaned to private schools practicing racial discrimination. In *Runyon v. McCrary* (427 U.S. 160: 1976), the Court held that private schools could be prohibited from racially exclusive admissions practices. The *Bob Jones* case is of greater significance in that it establishes the priority of combating racial discrimination over religious beliefs and recognizes the broad governmental authority vested in administrative agencies to pursue that policy. A year after *Bob Jones*, the Court muddied the pond by using the requirement for standing to set aside a suit brought by black parents challenging the tax exemptions enjoyed by racially discriminatory private schools. In *Allen v. Wright* (468 U.S. 737: 1984), the Court held that plaintiffs in such suits must show direct injury traceable to the school's discriminatory conduct. The allegation that progress toward desegregation was impaired by the exemption was viewed by the Court as too indirect and speculative to satisfy the requirements for standing to sue.

## Affirmative Action

***Local #28 of the Sheet Metal Workers' International v. Equal Employment Opportunity Commission*, 473 U.S. 000, 106 S.Ct. 3019, 92 L.Ed. 2d 344 (1986)**    Sanctioned the use of affirmative action as a means of addressing past racial discrimination. This case involved a court-ordered minority membership target for a union local. Membership in the union came when a person completed a four-year apprenticeship training program. As early as 1964, the local was ordered to cease and desist from its racially discriminatory practices and directed to implement objective standards for selecting apprentices. A series of follow-up proceedings took place, each of which proved ineffective. Recognizing that the record against the local was "replete with instances of bad faith attempts to prevent or delay affirmative action," a federal district court invoked provisions of Title VII of the Civil Rights Act of 1964 and imposed a 29 percent nonwhite membership goal. The local was subsequently determined to be in noncompliance and twice found in contempt of court and fined. The fine of $150,000 was to be placed in a fund designed to increase nonwhite membership in the apprenticeship program. The local and its apprenticeship committee, supported by the Solicitor General of the United States, challenged these rulings with the argument that the membership goal and fund exceeded the scope of remedies available under Title VII. They extended "race conscious preferences" to individuals who are not identified victims of the local's unlawful discrimination. In a 5–4 decision, the Supreme Court rejected the argument and upheld the order containing the membership goal and fund requirements. Speaking for the

Court, Justice Brennan said that Congress clearly intended to vest district courts with broad discretion to award appropriate equitable relief to remedy unlawful discrimination. The availability of race-conscious affirmative relief for violations of Title VII furthers the broad purposes underlying the statute. Such affirmative race-conscious relief may be the only means available to assure equality of employment opportunities and to eliminate those discriminatory practices and devices that have "fostered racially stratified job environments to the disadvantage of minority citizens." In most situations, courts need only order an employer to cease discriminatory practices and make the appropriate award of relief to victimized individuals. In some cases, however, it may be necessary to require an employer or union to take affirmative steps to end discrimination effectively. If an employer or union has been involved with particularly long-standing or egregious discrimination, compelling it to hire or admit to membership qualified minorities roughly in proportion to the number of qualified minorities in the workforce may be the only effective way to ensure the full enjoyment of the rights protected by Title VII. Justice O'Connor agreed that federal courts may, under certain circumstances, order preferential relief benefiting individuals who are not the actual victims of discrimination as a remedy for Title VII violations. Chief Justice Burger and Justice Rehnquist believed that remedies should be confined to the actual victims of discrimination. Justice White did not subscribe to that proposition, but he saw the district court order establishing a racial quota which the Court had historically rejected. *See also* EQUAL PROTECTION CLAUSE, p. 313; *REGENTS OF THE UNIVERSITY OF CALIFORNIA V. BAKKE* (438 U.S. 265: 1978), p. 337; REVERSE DISCRIMINATION, p. 447.

*Significance*     *Local #28 of the Sheet Metal Workers' International v. Equal Employment Opportunity Commission* (92 L.Ed. 2d 344: 1986) was one of three important workplace affirmative action rulings made by the Burger Court during the 1985–86 term. The first was *Wygant v. Jackson Board of Education* (90 L.Ed. 2d 260: 1986) in which the Court determined that the remedy for past discrimination may make it necessary to take race into account even if "innocent persons may be called upon to bear some of the burden of the remedy." In a concurring opinion, Justice O'Connor said that addressing past discrimination is a "sufficiently weighty state interest to warrant the remedial use of a carefully constructed affirmative action program." The Court rejected the view advanced by the Reagan Administration that racial preference in employment was to be used only to remedy specifically named victims. Despite the endorsement of affirmative action in general, however, the five-justice majority refused to allow the layoff of white teachers to preserve the employment of less senior black teachers. In order to do so, the racial preference required a showing of compelling state interest. Given the fact that the Jackson school district was not found to have discriminated against blacks in hiring teachers, the compelling interest test was not met. The other important 1986 affirmative action ruling came in *Local #93 of the International Association of Firefighters v. City of Cleveland* (92 L.Ed. 2d 405: 1986). In this case, the city of Cleveland had agreed to resolve employment discrimination suits brought by black and Hispanic firefighters by promising to promote black and Hispanic workers one-for-one with whites, notwithstanding seniority and test performance. In a 6–3 decision, the Court ruled that Title VII does not preclude federal courts from approving such agreements. The Court saw such consent decrees as a preferred means of achieving voluntary compliance with Title VII.

## Gerrymandering

*Davis v. Bandemer*, **478 U.S. 000, 106 S. Ct. 2797, 92 L.Ed. 2d 85 (1986)** Ruled that claims of political gerrymandering are justiciable. *Davis v. Bandemer* focused on a challenge to Indiana's reapportionment plan devised after the 1980 census. The plan called for a mixture of single and multimember districts to elect the state House of Representatives. Democrats challenged the plan, alleging that it was intentionally disadvantageous and thus violated their right to equal protection of the laws. Results from the 1982 election did show a dilution of the Democratic vote. Democratic House candidates received 51.9 percent of the vote cast statewide, but won only 43 of the 100 seats in the House. A federal district court invalidated the reapportionment plan and enjoined the state from holding further elections using it. The Supreme Court reversed the lower court in a 7–2 decision, but it ruled 6–3 that gerrymandering claims are justiciable even where the plan under challenge meets the one person–one vote standard. Justice White delivered the opinion of the Court. He said the case presented none of the identifying characteristics of a nonjusticiable political question. Neither did it present issues where there were no judicially discernible and manageable standards by which to decide the case. The suit claimed that "each political group in a state should have the same chance to elect representatives of its choice as any other political group." Even though the one person–one vote standard does not apply, the issue is indeed one of representation, and "we decline to hold that such claims are never justiciable." Chief Justice Burger and Justices Rehnquist and O'Connor maintained that partisan gerrymandering challenges were categorically nonjusticiable. Justice White said that an equal protection violation requires a threshold showing of discriminatory vote dilution. The mere fact that an apportionment plan makes it more difficult for a particular group in a particular district to elect the representatives of its choice does not render that scheme constitutionally infirm. Unconstitutional vote dilution, either on an individual district or statewide level, requires demonstration beyond a mere lack of proportional representation. Unconstitutional discrimination occurs "only when the electoral system is arranged in a manner that will consistently degrade a voter's or a group of voters' influence on the political process as a whole." The principal question in reviewing gerrymandering allegations is whether or not a particular group has been "unconstitutionally denied its chance to effectively influence the political process." A finding of unconstitutionality must be supported by evidence of "continued frustration of the will of a majority of the voters or effective denial to a minority of voters of a fair chance to influence the political process." Relying on a single election to prove unconstitutional discrimination was viewed as unsatisfactory. Justices Powell and Stevens were critical of this single standard. They preferred a multifactor analysis, and on such basis would have upheld the lower court's finding of discrimination. *See also* APPORTIONMENT, p. 384; JUSTICIABILITY, p. 432, POLITICAL QUESTION, p. 442; *MOBILE V. BOLDEN* (446 U.S. 55: 1980), p. 346.

*Significance*      Although the Court refused to support judicial invalidation of an Indiana reapportionment plan, it ruled in *Davis v. Bandemer* (92 L.Ed. 2d 85: 1986) that gerrymandering is subject to constitutional challenge. The Court also made challenge of electoral practices and districting schemes more vulnerable in *Thornburg v. Gingles* (92 L.Ed. 2d 25: 1986). To better understand this ruling, it is necessary to backtrack to *Mobile v. Bolden* (446 U.S. 55: 1980). In *Bolden*, the Court held that plaintiffs in cases that allege the dilution of minority votes must demonstrate that a disputed practice or plan was conceived or operated as a purposeful device to further racial discrimination. The *Bolden* decision prompted amendment of Section 2 of the Voting Rights Act in 1982. The amendment changed the focus from intent to electoral outcomes in assessing discrimination. A unanimous Court ruled in *Gingles* that a Section 2 claim is not foreclosed simply because some minority candidates have been successful. A plan that dilutes minority votes cannot be defended on the ground that it "sporadically and serendipitously benefits minority voters." The Court then fragmented on the criteria to be used in Section 2 cases. Writing for five members of the Court, Justice Brennan offered a three-element standard for establishing a violation. First, minority challengers must show that they are large and geographically compact enough to constitute a majority of voters in the district. Second, the challenging group must show that it votes cohesively. Third, the minority group must be able to demonstrate that a majority of whites usually vote to defeat the minority's preferred candidates. If a challenging group cannot respond to these criteria, the challenged plan or practice cannot be found responsible for the inability of minority voters to elect their candidates.

## Age

*Massachusetts Board of Retirement v. Murgia*, **427 U.S. 307, 96 S.Ct. 2562, 49 L.Ed. 2d 520 (1976)** Upheld a mandatory retirement age of 50 for uniformed police officers against Fourteenth Amendment challenge. *Massachusetts Board of Retirement v. Murgia* illustrates the rationality test for invalidating classifications. In reviewing challenged classification schemes, the Supreme Court has used different evaluative criteria or standards, the least stringent of which is the rationality test. It would invalidate classifications only if they are arbitrary and have no demonstrable justification. The rationality test is typically used in reviewing age-based classifications. In *Murgia*, a provision of state law required that uniformed state police officers retire at age 50. Key to the Court's holding in the case was the criteria used to assess the mandatory retirement policy. Murgia argued that the age classification was a "suspect class" and entitled to a "strict scrutiny" review, a more stringent review than that associated with the rationality test. The Court disagreed and held that Murgia did not belong to a suspect class. His claim could be reviewed using the rationality test. In a 7–1 decision, Justice Stevens not participating, the Court upheld the mandatory retirement law and determined that the strict scrutiny approach should be used only when the classification impermissibly interferes with the exercise of a fundamental right or operates to the particular disadvantage of a suspect class. In the Court's view the Massachusetts policy involved neither situation. It proceeded using the rational basis standard, a relatively relaxed criterion reflecting the Court's awareness that the drawing of lines creating distinctions is peculiarly and unavoidably a legislative task. The legislature's actions are presumed to be valid under this approach, and "perfection in making the necessary classification is neither possible nor necessary." In this instance, the legislature sought "to protect the public by assuring the physical preparedness of its uniformed police." Given the fact that physical ability generally declines with age, the Court found the mandatory retirement policy rationally related to the state's objective. It concluded by saying the choice of policy by Massachusetts may not be the best means, nor that a more just and humane system could not be devised, but under the rational basis test the enactment did not deny equal protection. Justice Marshall dissented from the use of the less demanding test because of its failure to sufficiently safeguard equal protection interests. He would have preferred a flexible standard that would have examined more carefully the means chosen by Massachusetts. To Justice Marshall, the means chosen "forced retirement of officers at age 50 and is therefore so overinclusive that it must fall." *See also* CLASSIFICATION, p. 394; EQUAL PROTECTION CLAUSE, p. 313; FOURTEENTH AMENDMENT, p. 412.

*Significance    Massachusetts Board of Retirement v. Murgia* (427 U.S. 307: 1976) stated that a mandatory retirement policy for uniformed police officers was rational. Soon after *Murgia*, the Court upheld a mandatory retirement policy for Foreign Service Officers in *Vance v. Bradley* (440 U.S. 93: 1979). Again the Court found a retirement policy rationally related to the legislative goal of assuring the professional capacity of persons holding critical public service positions. In this case, Foreign Service Officers have to undergo special rigors associated with overseas duty. Justice Marshall dissented and reiterated his call for a more demanding standard in reviewing such legislation. Not all age discrimination suits have been unsuccessful, however. In *Trans World Airlines, Inc. v. Thurston* (469 U.S. 111: 1984), the Court unanimously held that an airline's policy of not permitting the automatic transfer of age-disqualified captains to other positions with the company was a violation of the Age Discrimination in Employment Act of 1967. The *Thurston* decision was soon followed by two other important rulings on the same federal law. In *Western Air Lines, Inc. v. Criswell* (86 L.Ed. 2d 321: 1985), the Court unanimously held that an airline could not require mandatory retirement of flight engineers at age 60. Unlike the situation of pilots and copilots where age was considered a bona fide occupational qualification, the Court felt that flight engineers could be individually assessed rather than subjected to blanket early retirement rules. In *Johnson v. Mayor and City Council of Baltimore* (86 L.Ed. 2d 286: 1985), a unanimous Court also refused to permit a municipality to require mandatory retirement of firefighters at age 55. Key to this decision was the Court's rejection of Baltimore's contention that Congress had approved mandatory retirement when it retained such a policy for federal firefighters at the time it amended the statute in 1978. The Court held that retention of the provision was only for expediency and did not reflect a legislative judgment that youth was a bona fide qualification for the job. In *Equal Employment Opportunity Commission v. Wyoming* (460 U.S. 226: 1983), the Court ruled that state and local governments are not immune from provisions of the Age Discrimination in Employment Act. This Act prohibits employer discrimination against any employee or potential employee because of age. The Court made it clear, however, that the judgment did not compel a state to abandon policies that can demonstrate age as a bona fide occupational qualification. Central to the decisions in both *Murgia* and *Bradley* was the holding that compulsory retirement would better ensure good job performance by limiting the age of employees. Both cases sought to maximize the physical capabilities of persons performing certain functions. The question of physical qualifications for professional training programs was addressed in *Southeastern Community College v. Davis* (440 U.S. 979: 1979). Davis sought admission to a registered nursing program at a state community college despite a hearing disability. She was denied admission. She filed suit under the Rehabilitation Act of 1973 which prohibits discrimination against "an otherwise qualified handicapped person, solely by reason of his handicap." The Court unanimously held that an educational institution may impose reasonable physical qualifications for admission to a clinical training program. The Court did not require the college to make program adjustments to accommodate handicapped persons.

## Gender: Employment

*County of Washington v. Gunther,* **450 U.S. 907, 101 S.Ct. 2242, 68 L.Ed. 2d 751 (1981)**     Held that Title VII of the Civil Rights Act of 1964 covered more than equal pay for equal work claims. *County of Washington v. Gunther* allowed the Court to clarify the relationship between two federal enactments treating sex-based wage discrimination. Title VII of the Civil Rights Act of 1964 barred employment discrimination. The Equal Pay Act of 1963 prohibited wage differentials based on sex for persons performing equivalent work. Title VII contained a reference to the Equal Pay Act through a provision of the Bennett amendment, which exempted from the Equal Pay Act differences in wage stemming from seniority, merit, or work quantity. The question in *Gunther* was whether or not the Bennett amendment made Title VII and the Equal Pay Act coextensive relative to wage discrimination, or whether Title VII provided broader protection than situations in which unequal pay for equal work were involved. Gunther, a female guard at a county jail, brought suit under Title VII claiming wage disparity between male and female guards for substantially similar, but not identical, work. In a 5–4 decision, the Court ruled that the Bennett amendment permitted Title VII litigation to go beyond equal pay for equal work claims. Justice Brennan's opinion stressed that the objective of the Bennett amendment was to make the two statutes compatible by specifying some affirmative defenses which would apply in situations where pay disparities existed for equal work. To confine Title VII to the equal work standard of the Equal Pay Act would mean that a woman who is discriminatorily underpaid could obtain no relief, no matter how egregious the discrimination might be, unless her employer also employed a man in an equal job in the same establishment at a higher rate of pay. The majority rejected the view that Congress had intended the Bennett amendment "to insulate such blatantly discriminatory practices from judicial redress under Title VII." Rather, Title VII was used by Congress "to strike at the entire spectrum of disparate treatment of men and women resulting from sex stereotypes." Chief Justice Burger and Justices Stewart and Powell joined in a vigorous dissent written by Justice Rehnquist. The dissenters felt the intent of Congress in Title VII was that claims of gender-based wage discrimination were contingent on a showing of equal work. The minority was highly critical of the majority's judicial activism. Justice Rehnquist said the Court's decision was based on the majority's "unshakable belief that any other result would be unsound public policy." He charged that "the Court is obviously more interested in the consequences of its decision than in discerning the intention of Congress," and that "the Court relies wholly on what it believes Congress should have enacted." The decision was "simply a case where the Court superimposed on Title VII a gloss of its own choosing." *See also* CIVIL RIGHTS ACT OF 1964, p. 393; EQUAL PROTECTION CLAUSE, p. 313; *FRONTIERO V. RICHARDSON* (411 U.S. 677: 1973), p. 359; *ROSTKER V. GOLDBERG* (453 U.S. 57: 1981), p. 361.

*Significance*        *County of Washington v. Gunther* (450 U.S. 907: 1981) held that Title VII challenges of sex-based wage discrimination are not limited to claims of unequal pay for equal work. While the Court explicitly said that its decision did not embrace the comparable work concept, *Gunther* did mean that women bringing wage discrimination suits need only show that gender was used in a discriminatory fashion in setting a rate of pay. *Gunther* also reflected the broadening view of the Burger Court about what constitutes sex discrimination. In *Geduldig v. Aiello* (417 U.S. 484: 1974), the Court had allowed a state disability insurance program to exempt coverage of wage losses from normal pregnancies. Rather than finding a classification by sex, the Court held that the two classes were divided on the basis of pregnancy, and the nonpregnant class consisted of both men and women. Three subsequent cases, however, found the Court moving away from the *Geduldig* position. In *Newport News Shipbuilding and Dry Dock Company v. EEOC* (462 U.S. 669: 1983), the Court struck down a health plan which did not provide the same pregnancy coverage for wives of male employees as it provided for female employees. In *Los Angeles Department of Water and Power v. Manhart* (435 U.S. 702: 1978), the Court held that requiring female employees to make higher contributions to retirement programs than men violated Title VII, despite the statistical probability that a woman would collect more retirement benefits because of greater longevity. The counterpart to *Manhart* came in *Arizona Governing Committee for Tax Deferred Annuity and Deferred Compensation Plans v. Norris* (463 U.S. 1073: 1983), in which the Court invalidated an employer-sponsored retirement plan that provided smaller benefits to women by using sex-based actuarial tables reflecting greater longevity for women. The Court said the classification of employees on the basis of sex was no more permissible at the pay-out stage of a retirement plan than at the pay-in stage. In *Hishon v. King & Spalding* (81 L.Ed. 2d 59: 1984), the Court unanimously held that law firms may not discriminate on the basis of gender in making decisions on promotion to partnership. The Court rejected two arguments advanced by the law firm. First, the firm contended that such promotion decisions as this were exempt from the job discrimination provisions of Title VII. Second, the firm maintained that the right of association insulated partnership decisions. The Court disagreed on both points. In *Roberts v. United States Jaycees* (82 L.Ed. 2d 462: 1984), the Court upheld the application of a state antidiscrimination law which forced an organization to accept women into its membership. The Court found that the state's interest in promoting gender equality prevailed over the organization's expression and association interests.

## Gender: Title IX

*Grove City College v. Bell*, **465 U.S. 555, 104 S.Ct. 1211, 79 L.Ed. 2d 516 (1984)**     Held that Title IX prohibitions against sex discrimination apply to private institutions through the fact that enrolled students receive federal education grants. *Grove City College v. Bell* also limited the scope of Title IX by ruling that the statute's language does not apply to an educational institution in it entirety, but only to the specific programs through which federal aid is received. Title IX of the Educational Amendments of 1972 prohibits sex discrimination" in any education program or activity receiving Federal financial assistance." There is also a provision that permits any federal agency administering assistance programs to secure compliance by terminating federal aid if compliance is not forthcoming. Grove City College, a private institution, accepted no federal assistance directly nor did it administer any federal student grants. It did enroll a number of students who received federal educational grants. When the college refused to sign an assurance of compliance with Title IX, the Department of Education sought to terminate the grants awarded to students of the college on the grounds that Grove City was a recipient of federal assistance, however indirectly. The Supreme Court unanimously ruled that Title IX did apply to Grove City through the student grant program. The Court qualified the holding, however, by saying that receipt of the grant by some students did not require application of Title IX on an institution-wide basis. The holding affected only the college's financial aid program. The Court split 6–3 on this issue, the majority opinion delivered by Justice White. He said the case addressed two important aspects of the scope and reach of Title IX and the regulations established by the Department of Education pursuant to Title IX. First, the Court rejected Grove City's contention that by its refusal to accept direct federal and state assistance, it had preserved its institutional autonomy from Title IX. The Court found that where students finance their education with Basic Educational Opportunity Grants (BEOGs), a centerpiece element of the Educational Amendments of 1972, an institution's programs are drawn into the coverage of Title IX. Congress had recognized discrimination in the administration of financial aid in education, and it sought to address the problem with BEOGs. The Court said it would be "anomalous" to find that one of the primary components of the comprehensive package of federal aid was not intended to trigger coverage under Title IX. The linchpin of Grove City's argument was the direct-indirect distinction, but the Court saw no support in the text of the law for such a distinction. The Court said the language of the relevant section (901[a]) was "all inclusive terminology" covering all forms of federal educational aid, direct or indirect. The Court also noted that Title IX was patterned after Title VI of the Civil Rights Act of 1964. Title VI envisioned the initiation of coverage with receipt of federal aid, and since Congress approved identical language when Title IX was adopted, the Court had no reason to believe that those who voted for Title IX intended a different result. The Court then turned to the more crucial problem of identifying the program or activity that actually received the federal assistance. The Court read the appropriate sections of the law as subject to program-specific limitations. It rejected the view that "Grove City itself is a 'program or activity' that may be regulated in its entirety." In addition to what it saw as clear program-specific language, the Court said there was no evidence that the aid received by Grove City students resulted in diversion of funds from the college's student aid fund to other uses. Neither did the Court find the student aid analogous to a nonearmarked direct grant that an institution might use for whatever purpose it desired. The purpose of the grant was to enable students to get an education, not to increase institutional revenues. While the student grants ultimately find their way into Grove City's general operating budget, that did not create regulatory authority to follow federally aided students from classroom to classroom, building to building, or activity to activity. Thus, while

Grove City could be required to execute an Assurance of Compliance for its student aid program, under threat of termination of student grants, it could not be required to apply Title IX provisions institution-wide. Justices Brennan, Marshall, and Stevens dissented on the second point, each for different reasons. Justice Brennan said the decision "conveniently ignored controlling indicia of congressional intent." He referred to the "absurdity" of the decision's practical effect. He feared the decision permits gender discrimination in mathematics classes, for example, even though affected students are supported by federal funds. "If anything about Title IX were ever certain," it is that discrimination practices "were meant to be prohibited by the statute" on an institutionwide basis. *See also* CIVIL RIGHTS ACT OF 1964, p. 393; EQUAL PROTECTION CLAUSE, p. 313.

*Significance*    The Court's decision in *Grove City College v. Bell* (465 U.S. 555: 1984) severely limited the scope of Title IX and reversed a decade of interpretation that the law reached entire institutions. The Court's judgment on this point essentially upheld a Reagan Administration initiative which began to confine Title IX administratively. As recently as 1982, the Court had opted not to make restrictive interpretations of Title IX. In *North Haven Board of Education v. Bell* (456 U.S. 512: 1982), for example, the Court held that Title IX prohibited sex discrimination in the employment practices of institutions receiving federal assistance. In doing so, the Court upheld an agency-ordered termination of funds to a school district, even though the language of Title IX does not explicitly extend to employment situations. The implications of *Grove City* are not immediately clear. On the one hand, it could be the beginning of a more comprehensive effort to confine the scope of civil rights regulations, including those aimed at racial discrimination in specific program subsets of larger institutions. On the other hand, the effect of the decision may be reversed legislatively because the Court's decision rests on its interpretation of congressional intent. Subsequent legislative action could correct any judicial misinterpretation that may be involved.

## Gender: Benevolent

*Kahn v. Shevin*, **416 U.S. 351, 94 S.Ct. 1734, 40 L.Ed. 2d 189 (1973)**    Upheld a state statute which provided a property tax exemption to widows, but not widowers. *Kahn v. Shevin* explored the fact that not all gender-based classifications convey disabilities to women. A number of enactments use gender as a benevolent classification, and *Kahn* allowed such a preferential policy. A Florida statute provided widows with an annual $500 exemption on property taxes. No similar benefit existed for widowers. The Supreme Court found the classification permissible in a 6–3 decision. Justice Douglas wrote the brief opinion of the Court. He noted that "the financial difficulties confronting the lone woman in Florida or in any other State exceed those facing the man." Whether the cause was overt discrimination or "the socialization process of a male dominated culture," a woman finds the job market inhospitable. Justice Douglas referred to data showing income disparities between males and females. This disparity was likely to be exacerbated for the widow. Unlike the male, the widow will be thrust into "a job market with which she is unfamiliar, and in which, because of her former economic dependency, she will have fewer skills to offer." The tax exemption was designed to further the policy of "cushioning the financial impact of spousal loss upon the sex for whom that loss imposes a disproportionately heavy burden." The Court differentiated this situation from that of *Frontiero v. Richardson* (411 U.S. 677: 1973), where benefits were granted on a gender basis solely for administrative convenience. The differentiation that favored females over males in granting the tax exemption in *Kahn* was a reasonable rather than an arbitrary distinction. States are to be permitted large leeway in making such classifications. Justices Brennan, White, and Marshall dissented. They argued that gender-based classifications are suspect and require more justification than the state offered. The dissenters also felt the statute was "plainly overinclusive," and that the state should have been required to prove that its interests could not have been served by a more precisely tailored statute or by use of feasible and less drastic means. For the dissenters, Florida could have advanced the interest of ameliorating the effect of past economic discrimination against women without categorically excluding males or including widows of substantial economic means. See also BENEVOLENT CLASSIFICATION, p. 388; *COUNTY OF WASHINGTON V. GUNTHER* (452 U.S. 161: 1981), p. 363; EQUAL PROTECTION CLAUSE, p. 313; *FRONTIERO V. RICHARDSON* (411 U.S. 677: 1973), p. 359; *ROSTKER V. GOLDBERG* (453 U.S. 57: 1981), p. 361.

*Significance*     *Kahn v. Shevin* (416 U.S. 351: 1973) upheld benevolent classifications. In *Califano v. Webster* (430 U.S. 313: 1977), the Court allowed a provision of the Social Security Act which permitted a woman to exclude more low-earning years than a male could exclude in calculating an average wage for use in the benefit formula. The objective of the provision was "the permissible one of redressing our society's longstanding disparate treatment of women." The Court also upheld a gender-based differential requiring mandatory discharge of naval officers who failed to be promoted within a specified period of time in *Schlesinger v. Ballard* (419 U.S. 498: 1975). Women were permitted four more years to gain promotion because women officers were not "similarly situated" to men. They had fewer opportunities to gain the needed professional service required for promotion. Nevertheless, the Court has found some benevolent gender classifications actually to be punitive and therefore invalid. In *Weinberger v. Wiesenfeld* (420 U.S. 636: 1975), for example, the Court found that social security survivor benefits for widows with minor children discriminated against women in that their compulsory social security contributions produced less protection for their survivors than the comparable contributions of men. Using the same reasoning, the Court set aside dependency requirements in the Federal Old-Age, Survivors, and Disability Insurance Benefits Program in *Califano v. Goldfarb* (430 U.S. 199: 1977). From the perspective of the two wage earners, the Act "plainly disadvantages women contributors as compared with similarly situated men." Following *Goldfarb,* Congress repealed the dependency requirement, but adopted a pension offset provision to soften the fiscal impact on the Social Security Trust Fund. The offset reduced benefits, but Congress exempted certain persons from the offset requirement if they had retired or were about to retire at the time the offset policy was adopted. While the exemption protected the financial interests of these people, it also had the effect of extending the gender classification invalidated in *Goldfarb.* The Court unanimously upheld the exemption in *Heckler v. Matthews* (465 U.S. 728: 1984). In another social security benefits decision, the Court said in *Bowen v. Owens* (90 L.Ed. 2d 316: 1986) that Congress could extend survivor benefits to widowed spouses who remarry while denying the same benefits to a surviving spouse who had been divorced from the decedent. The Court ruled that Congress had discretion to concentrate limited federal resources in places where the need was greatest. Since divorced spouses did not enter remarriage with the same level of dependency on the wage earner's account as widowed persons, the Court reasoned it was acceptable for Congress to treat these groups differently after remarriage. Finally, in *Orr v. Orr* (440 U.S. 268: 1979), the Court voided an Alabama statute authorizing alimony payments to women but not to men. Justice Brennan suggested that benevolent gender classification carries "the inherent risk of reinforcing stereotypes about the proper place of women." Even compensatory objectives must be carefully tailored. Here the state's purpose could be as well served by a gender-neutral classification as by one that classifies by gender. The latter carries with it the baggage of sexual stereotypes.

## RIGHT OF PRIVACY

### Abortion Regulation

*Thornburgh v. American College of Obstetricians and Gyne-cologists*, **476 U.S. 000, 106 S.Ct. 2169, 90 L.Ed. 2d 779 (1986)** Reaffirmed a woman's constitutional right to an abortion. *Thornburgh v. American College of Obstetricians and Gynecologists* involved a challenge to a state abortion control statute. The authors of the statute did not dispute the fact that the law was designed to discourage elective abortions. Suit was brought by an organization of obstetricians and gynecologists as well as various individuals. They alleged the statute was incompatible with *Roe v. Wade* (410 U.S. 113: 1973), which established a woman's legal right to an abortion. The challenged provisions of the statute fell into three main categories. The first required that all women give informed consent before an abortion. This required that all women be told of the comparative risks of abortion and full-term pregnancy, the medical assistance benefits available for full-term pregnancies, the legal recourse for obtaining support from the father, and the possible detrimental physical and psychological effects of having an abortion. Women were also to be told of the characteristics of the fetus in two-week gestational increments. The second category of regulations involved reporting. All physicians were required to report a variety of information about each woman, the abortion, and the non-viability of the fetus. While the reports were not to be deemed public records, they were accessible for public inspection and copying. Third, the law required all physicians performing abortions after a point when the fetus could be viable to exercise the degree of care required to preserve the fetus. The attendance of a second physician was necessary in all instances where viability was possible. A United States District Court denied injunctive relief, but was reversed by the Court of Appeals which found the statute unconstitutional. The Supreme Court affirmed the latter ruling. Justice Blackmun wrote the majority opinion. He began by reaffirming the basic position of *Roe v. Wade*. Despite the numerous attempts to restrict the exercise of a woman's right of choice, Blackmun stated that the constitutional principles that provided the basis for *Roe* "still provide the compelling reason for recognizing the constitutional dimensions of a woman's right to decide whether to end her pregnancy." The states are simply not free, under the guise of protecting maternal health or potential life, to intimidate women into continuing pregnancies. Close analysis of the statute's provisions shows that they wholly subordinate constitutional privacy interests and concerns with maternal health in an effort to deter a woman from making a decision that, with her physician, is hers to make. Blackmun characterized the informational requirements as "poorly disguised elements of discouragement for the abortion decision." He called the provision requiring dissemination of specific printed materials an "outright attempt to wedge" the state's antiabortion message into the privacy of the patient-physician dialogue. The reporting requirements were found impermissible because they "raise the spectre of public exposure." The decision to terminate a pregnancy is an intensely private one that must be protected in a way that assures anonymity. A woman and her physician will necessarily be more reluctant to choose an abortion if there exists a possibility that her decision and her identity will become known publicly. The second-physician attendance requirement where possible fetus viability exists was struck down because it addressed no medical emergency. It simply chilled the performance of late abortions. Blackmun concluded by saying the Constitution recognizes that a certain private sphere of individual liberty will be kept largely beyond the reach of government. Few decisions are more "personal and intimate, more properly private, or more basic to individual dignity and autonomy" than the abortion decision. Four justices dissented. Justices White and Rehnquist repeated the position they articulated in *Roe v. Wade*. Justice O'Connor said that abortion regulations should generally be upheld as long as they bear a rational relationship to the legitimate purpose of promoting maternal health and protection of the fetus. Chief Justice Burger joined the minority, characterizing the majority ruling as embracing the idea of abortion on demand, something not intended by *Roe v. Wade*. *See also* RIGHT OF PRIVACY, p. 316; *ROE V. WADE* (410 U.S. 113: 1973), p. 371; *CITY OF AKRON V. AKRON CENTER FOR REPRODUCTIVE HEALTH, INC.* (462 U.S. 416: 1983), p. 372.

*Significance*     The statute reviewed in *Thornburgh v. American College of Obstetricians and Gynecologists* (90 L.Ed. 2d 779: 1986) closely resembled the law struck down in *City of Akron v. Akron Center for Reproductive Health, Inc.* (462 U.S. 416: 1983). In that case, however, the margin against state regulation of abortion was 6–3 with Chief Justice Burger voting with the majority. Between *Akron* and *Thornburgh*, the Reagan Administration strongly urged the overruling of *Roe v. Wade*. While reversal did not happen in *Thornburgh*, the margin became extremely thin. Two other 1986 cases are also relevant in this subject area. *Thornburgh* was actually the second abortion case argued during the 1985–86 term. A similar Illinois statute was to be reviewed in *Diamond v. Charles* (90 L.Ed. 2d 584: 1986), but the Court dismissed the appeal on the grounds that the physician supporting the state regulations did not have standing. The action left undisturbed a lower court ruling striking the statute. The second relevant case, *Bowen v. American Hospital Association* (90 L.Ed. 2d 584: 1986), was known as the "Baby Doe" case. The Reagan Administration had sought to intervene in cases involving treatment of seriously handicapped infants. The asserted statutory basis for such intervention was Section 504 of the Rehabilitation Act of 1973. In a 5–3 decision, the Court said the act did not give the Secretary of Health and Human Services authority to offer unsolicited advice to those persons faced with "difficult treatment decisions concerning handicapped children." Intervention under the act could not occur without evidence that a hospital refused treatment requested by a child's parents. Nothing authorizes the secretary to dispense with the law's focus on discrimination.

## Definition of Family

*Moore v. City of East Cleveland*, **431 U.S. 494, 97 S.Ct. 1932, 52 L.Ed. 2d 531 (1977)**    Ruled that a municipality through a zoning ordinance did not have authority to restrict occupancy of a private home to persons defined as a family. *Moore v. City of East Cleveland* involved an ordinance that limited occupancy of a dwelling unit to members of a "single family." The zone of privacy issue involved in the case had provided the basis for numerous challenges of legislation since *Griswold v. Connecticut* (381 U.S. 479: 1965, p. 369). Most successful applications of the invasion of privacy approach have been in situations where matters of family were involved in some way. In the East Cleveland ordinance, "family" was defined very narrowly to include essentially parents and children. Moore lived in her home with her son and two grandsons. She was found in violation of the ordinance because the grandsons were cousins rather than brothers. Although the Court could not agree on common language, a five-justice majority found the ordinance unconstitutional. The opinion of the Court was written by Justice Powell, who characterized the ordinance as "slicing deeply into the family itself." He said such an enactment compels the Court to act aggressively. "When a city undertakes such an intrusive regulation of the family, the usual judicial deference to the legislature is inappropriate." That posture was demanded because the Court had long recognized that freedom of personal choice in matters of marriage and family life is one of the liberties protected by the Due Process Clause of the Fourteenth Amendment. Justice Powell acknowledged that the family is not beyond regulation, but in doing so governmental interests must be very carefully examined, as well as the means chosen to advance those interests. The interests asserted by East Cleveland were served only marginally by the ordinance. Justice Powell noted the risk involved when "the judicial branch gives enhanced protection to certain substantive liberties without the guidance of more specific provisions of the Bill of Rights." Although history counsels caution and restraint as a general rule, it does not counsel abandonment. Nor does it require what the city urges, i.e., cutting off any protection of family rights at the first convenient boundary, the boundary of the nuclear family. Justice Brennan concurred and said the zoning power "is not a license for local communities to enact senseless and arbitrary restrictions which cut deeply into private areas of protected family life." He also charged that the ordinance was the imposition of "white suburbia's preference in patterns of family living," a preference reflecting "cultural myopia" and insensitivity to the concept of the extended family. Justices Stewart, White, and Rehnquist disagreed that the ordinance interfered with an aspect of family life deserving constitutional protection. The three did not feel that Moore's claim was sufficient for heightened protection under the Due Process Clause. Chief Justice Burger also dissented, but based his disagreement on the ground that Moore had not fully exhausted the administrative remedies available to her. *See also* FOURTEENTH AMENDMENT, p. 412; *GRISWOLD V. CONNECTICUT* (381 U.S. 479: 1965),.p. 369; RIGHT OF PRIVACY, p. 316.

*Significance*    *Moore v. City of East Cleveland* (431 U.S. 494: 1977) set aside an ordinance that attempted to restrict occupancy of a home to persons within the ordinance definition of a family. Prior to *Moore*, the Court had upheld a zoning ordinance in *Belle Terre v. Boraas* (416 U.S. 1: 1974), which limited land use to single-family dwellings. The ordinance defined family more broadly than the enactment in *Moore*, and the Court deferred to the permissible legislative objectives of regulating population density and preventing congestion and noise. In *Zablocki v. Redhail* (434 U.S. 374: 1978), the Court found that the right of privacy precluded interference with a person's desire to marry. A state statute required any person under an order to pay child support to obtain authorization to marry. Permission was contingent on showing that support obligations were current and that the children involved "would not likely thereafter become public charges." Redhail was denied a marriage license because he had failed to make support payments for a previously fathered child. The Court held the statute unconstitutional because it barred certain classes from ever marrying. They were "coerced into foregoing the right to marry." The right of privacy is limited to traditional marital relationships in *Doe v. Commonwealth Attorney for the City of Richmond* (425 U.S. 901: 1976). The Court summarily affirmed a three-judge district court dismissal of a privacy challenge to the use of a state sodomy statute against homosexuals. The lower court found that homosexuality was "obviously no portion of marriage, house, or family life," and that a state may impose criminal sanctions on conduct "even when committed in the home, in the promotion of morality and decency." The refusal to extend the right of privacy to homosexual conduct was amplified in the highly controversial ruling of *Bowers v. Hardwick* (92 L.Ed. 2d 140: 1986). In this case, the Court upheld a state law that criminalized consensual sodomy. The Court said that homosexuals had no right to engage in sodomy. In addition, the Court said that none of the previous right of privacy rulings involving family relationships, marriage, and procreation "bear any resemblance to the claimed constitutional right of homosexuals to engage in acts of sodomy that is asserted in this case." The Court also categorically rejected the contention that the previous right of privacy cases insulated private sexual conduct between consenting adults from state regulation. Neither does the fact that the conduct occurred in the privacy of a home immunize otherwise illegal conduct. Victimless crimes such as possession and use of illegal drugs, said the Court, "do not escape the law when they are committed at home." The same is true for sexual conduct. It would be difficult to limit the asserted right to homosexual conduct "while leaving exposed to prosecution adultery, incest, and other sexual crimes even though they are committed in the home. We are unwilling to start down that road."

# INDEX

Cross-references to dictionary entries are located in the text at the end of each definition paragraph. Page references in BOLD type indicate dictionary entries.